The Second Wiseman

A Quest for Liberty and Justice

Howard W. Wiseman

Wordminder Press

Norfolk VA

Published by:
Wordminder Press
PO Box 10438
Norfolk VA 23513-0438
www.WordminderPress.com
(757) 853-4788

Edited by Susan M. Andrus and D.D. Delaney.
Cover designed by Amy Jacoby.

Library of Congress Control Number: 2005930893

ISBN-10: 0-9729103-1-X
ISBN-13: 978-0-9729103-1-6

The following autobiography pays tribute to my parents, Frank and Ruth Wiseman, who are deceased but not forgotten in their children's eyes and especially in mine. At any rate they deserve the credit because if it were not for their faith, encouragement and values, I would not have had the experiences as outlined.

Table of Contents

PART 1 THE GREAT DEPRESSION

The Devastating Fire

In the early 1930s, my father located employment at the Viscose Company in Roanoke. He went to work at 10 p.m. and finished his work about 7 the following morning. He was quite happy to have gotten the job because a large number of people were out of work but not everyone was as happy as he about his having an income.

One night a pumping sound at the back door awakened him. This was the only door available at that time to enter the house. He came downstairs from his sleep at about 8 p.m. and asked about the noise. No one could answer his question, but when he opened the back door we smelled a gaseous substance, which had been sprayed under and around the door including the outside of the doorstep.

The odor was awful and it remained for hours, even with the door opened. But because of the cold, it was almost impossible to keep the door open.

We never learned why the gas was used on our house. Because the doors were never locked, the person could have come in and sprayed the gaseous substance over the floor without anyone knowing he was there. We usually gathered in the second room around the heater, where we children talked and played.

It must be remembered that neither we nor any of our neighbors had expensive items to be stolen. People however, could enter without being challenged. When my father asked the neighbors if they had heard or seen anyone around the house he received a negative answer, but they assured him they would continue to be on the lookout for any strange person roaming about. Unfortunately, we weren't vigilant enough.

Although we were playing and talking, we were not allowed to yell because my father needed his sleep. Besides that, he would become angry and give us a spanking if we woke him before it was time for him to get up for work. It happened several times before and we knew what would happen to us; therefore we were really quiet for small children. Following this episode we were extremely quiet but not quiet enough to prevent the fire that almost devastated us.

Our two-story wooden house burned to the ground one night during the winter of 1931 to 1932. The blaze awoke us around midnight. It burned so fast we barely got out alive. I recall the terror. A homemade wooden ladder my father left on the ground after working on the roof the day before saved us from total annihilation.

We later learned that the fire might have been set deliberately. But at that time the law enforcement people lacked the manpower and the expertise to do a thorough investigation. For the rest of my life, as if trying somehow to reconcile the terror of that night, I have set out on a quest to find justice for others and myself.

My father jumped from the porch roof to the ground and placed the ladder up to a window so that each of us could climb down to safety. The fire was so hot that our shins and the clothing covering them were scorched.

We all cried for help, trying to get someone to come to our rescue. It took almost forty-five minutes for the volunteers in the fire and rescue unit to get to the fire truck and bring it to our house.

We had no phone and do not know how the firemen heard of the fire. But then, we heard the siren at the fire station about five blocks from where we lived. It took only a few minutes for them to get to the fire after they got the fire truck started. But by then the old wooden structure we called home had completely burned to the ground.

My knickers, along with ironed clothing my mother had placed on a chair inside the window a few hours earlier, burned in the fire. The knickers had elastic around the leg bottom and the trousers bloused over my knees and down the leg as if they were too large for me to wear.

They were in style at that time and patterned after golf-type clothes. The loss of these clothes left me with nothing but the clothes I was wearing in bed. It was cold and windy that night and needless to say we all were traumatized.

As the saying goes, "When it rains, it pours," or if it can go wrong, it will with the least effort. This fire almost did us in physically and mentally because we lost everything, including hope.

We only survived because my father had left the ladder on the ground to be used the following day. All my life I have considered the possibility that our house and our bodies might have been burned beyond recognition without any knowledge of the culprit responsible for it.

Eventually there were six children – four boys and two girls, but at that time, only our parents and we three boys lived in the house. Our family was close and we became closer following the crash in 1929, as the Depression grew. We were forced to center on our family to find ways to provide for food and clothing and as time moved forward we had to alter plans on a daily basis.

I have asked myself many times how in the world we survived the cold mostly without heat and sometimes without food. We were fortunate in getting out of the building with nothing but hot skin on our legs and arms.

Later, we were told that our cries were heard but none of the neighbors could get to us fast enough to be of any help. In addition, aside from the tank carried on the fire truck, there was very little water available to extinguish fires.

Back then the pressure from the water main was the only thing available for the firemen to use and that was not forceful enough to extinguish a fire since the nearest fireplug was about a block away. The creek nearby did not have a sufficient water level to allow pumping even if the pumps were in operation on the fire trucks. It must have been at least six years before we had water mains and fireplugs near the house.

Following the fire, the only place for the family to go for shelter was to our grandparents' home. Somehow we got there but I do not recall how this happened. We may have walked the entire five miles to their house or maybe some kind person drove us. I do know that we could have used some of those burned up clothes, especially in those winter months.

We remained with my grandparents until my father could get funds to begin the reconstruction. Prior to the fire, he was beginning to have a small amount of work but he did not earn enough to buy the necessities for our family to live on. Those of us too young to do any work did menial tasks such as collecting fruits and vegetables to sell for whatever we could get in an effort to earn money for the family and ourselves. All of the money, fruits and food items we collected we took home for the family to eat or use to buy staple foods.

Each person was taught to share everything in an attempt to survive. Eventually, we prepared a garden space about fifty feet wide next to our house and we were taught to plant vegetables at the proper season. We worked the ground with a hoe to keep the weeds out.

Looking back on the entire episode of the fire and the dire poverty we suffered afterwards, I do not understand how any member of our family survived such a traumatic and costly experience. Since we were very young, we struggled to understand

We could manage with a minimum of clothing provided it was warm or we wore double layers; but we needed shoes. Many times we had to wear hand-me-down shoes of various sizes. If they were too large we stuffed them with paper or pieces of old clothing just to keep our feet warm and dry.

Neighbors and friends gave us clothing. My mother hand-sewed patched overalls for outerwear. She tried to get things for family members, doing without many things herself. I believe she sometimes went without food just so we could have something to eat. If our clothing was too large, she cut it to fit, sewing by hand. If it was too small, she cut it open and sewed in a patch to get a close fit.

My mother took the time and the patience to teach us boys how to repair certain articles of clothing. At this time she did not have a sewing machine nor did she have the funds to purchase one. She sewed by hand, cutting out pieces of cloth and sewing them to trousers or other garments in an effort to make us look presentable. We gladly accepted suit coats and worn shirts and wore them with pride even if they were torn or not the proper size.

It must have been in the late 1930s before I finally saved enough to buy a used overcoat. It cost ten or twelve dollars at a second-hand store. We had very few stores that contained clothing at a price affordable to folks such as us.

I recall that we walked to school through farmland. Some days we nearly froze before we got to school because the wind was too fierce for our thin clothing. All we had to wear were light, hand-me-down jackets, usually too small for us. We would really have appreciated a nice pair of shoes or better boots to keep our feet dry and warm but that never happened. However most of us made it through to 2000, for which we deserve a gold medal because we came a long way almost entirely on our own.

For times to be remembered as the good old days, there has to be joy and enthusiasm in the minds of those who lived them. I cannot say those times were as nice as some people have stated, but the lessons I learned molded me into the person I am today and I have no regrets. This can be demonstrated as I explain my early life in the late 1920s and early '30s.

I was born on November 18, 1921, in the town of Vinton, Virginia. Later when houses had numbers, our address was 411 Walnut Avenue in Roanoke County. The town of Vinton joins Roanoke, Virginia on the east and has remained a town as long as I can remember.

As a young person, I was amazed at the many things to learn and I must say that I attempted to learn most or all of them in a short time. I realize that some of the things I remember may not be the most important things to everyone; however I believe that some people may enjoy reading about the trials, tribulations, and experiences of my younger days.

We were young and looked at everything with a fresh outlook believing that we could conquer the world and everything we encountered. Youth has a way of overlooking the difficult areas of life by forging ahead without regard to dangers, thinking the end result is most important.

If I had to use one word to describe my childhood it would be sad. But it was not void of love from our parents. During our early years, many things happened which could not be explained to our small minds but we attempted to understand them from the information furnished by our parents, other family members and especially neighbors who knew a lot about the entire family.

Looking back on these times I do not understand how our parents explained our financial situation and lack of material things, which were needed to keep a family going. To put it bluntly, we were extremely poor with not even soap or water to wash the dirt from our bodies and no place to go and nowhere to hide our desperation.

One of the most anguished times was during Thanksgiving and on into Christmas when most children received gifts. (The Depression was just around the corner but we didn't know it.) Thanksgiving was a trying time to give thanks especially following a few disasters within the family circle that made it more difficult to find food for the entire family. One such disaster was the death of a baby brother just prior to Thanksgiving.

Many families had a Christmas tree beginning in early December with the celebration continuing on until the end of the month. We worked for others in the neighborhood to get pennies to buy food. Therefore, we had no funds to purchase Christmas trees or items that would be luxuries to us.

In fact, as I look back on the Christmas seasons, I remember them as among the most devastating times of my life. For one thing, everybody kept saying Santa Claus would bring us toys, fruit and anything we wished for. But even when we were very small, we wondered how in the world Santa could cover all the houses in the town and then go on to the large cities. When no answer was forthcoming, we became suspicious of this grand old man at Christmas time.

Most young persons, especially those who believed in Santa Claus looked upon the holidays as an exciting time. Young people looked forward to sugar plums, candy and lots of goodies to eat. We did not fit into that happy category because we lacked the

17

finances to buy anything. To be perfectly honest, we became soured, disappointed and frustrated at an early age because we could not look forward to the event that other young people anticipated.

The shopping area was confined to a country store unless one could travel to the city of Roanoke to shop, which we could not afford. At the local country store in the center of town, almost everything was ordered in by the owner, including cornmeal, which was a staple for us. At the drugstore the pharmacist compounded medicines by combining the ingredients from scratch. Most of the time he prepared the medication for Dr. Garthwright, the town's only doctor.

Dr. Garthwright was a kindly old gentleman who drove a horse and buggy to citizens' homes to treat them from his little black bag. He talked with us children about Santa Claus and all the good things he would deliver to us providing we were good and stayed out of trouble. Although he was specific about his belief in Santa Claus, he was never specific about our presents.

I could never figure out why he hung an iron weight reaching down to the ground around his horse's collar. As I became older, I realized that he used this to keep the horse from walking off with the buggy.

Later, Dr. Garthwright bought a small Model-T Ford, which he drove to visit his patients. He lived near the center of the town in a large wood-framed house where the sidewalks began and ended when they eventually were constructed.

The only things I remember receiving at Christmas were a piece of candy – chocolate fudge made by our mother – and an orange. We never had toys to play with; nor did we have bicycles as other kids had although once we had a tricycle loaned to us by one of the kids near our house.

I remember this tricycle very well. I tried to ride it on a rough area that had a concrete curb poured by the railroad company to contain a small body of water. As I attempted to ride over this curb, the tricycle overturned backward, causing me to fall and break my arm when it struck the curb.

This happened on a Saturday afternoon. Doctor Garthwright was not available. The only doctor was in Roanoke, about fifteen miles away. I do not recall how I was transported to the doctor but my arm and wrist had to be held straight until the doctor saw the break.

Before I left home with my father, my mother placed my arm on a pillow and instructed me not to move it but keep it in that position until the doctor examined it. The pain in my arm became almost unbearable. I cried. Trying to hold the pillow and my arm at the same time was too much.

Finally we arrived, climbed three flights of stairs and entered Dr. Roy M. Hoover's office. The only person in the office was the nurse, who told me that the doctor would get there in a short time. I immediately told her that I had to move my arm because it hurt but fearing it might cause more damage, she cautioned me not to.

That short time until the doctor arrived seemed like an eternity. I sat in a dimly lit room, which by itself was scary, waiting for what seemed to be hours. My arm hurt so much that I continued to cry. When the doctor finally got there he took one look at me and began to put a plaster cast on my arm.

It was dark when we left his office but I could not concentrate on anything except my hurting arm and the fact that I could not move it as I had before the break. I do not fault the doctor because he was nice. He tried not to hurt me further. He was regarded as the best orthopedic physician in the entire area and it was not his fault that I broke my arm.

I will always remember Dr. Hoover as the only physician available to set my broken arm. He never charged my family for that service. Maybe he knew we had no funds. Maybe my father told him of our dire condition. Later, he operated on my knees. I shall always remember him for this and for the many things he did for the community.

I later learned that many physicians regarded him highly not only in Roanoke but also throughout Virginia. He passed away in the 1960s, may he rest in peace. He was a God-fearing physician who healed and put the patients first.

The Second Wiseman

The Early Years

Prior to the fire when I was about ten years of age, my mother needed medical assistance. This was the first time I remember her being ill. She remained in bed for many months. This scared us. It seemed like forever. We knew that she and my father could not afford a doctor coming to the house and she was too ill to be moved or taken to a doctor even if transportation had been available. We had no knowledge of the difficulty and would not have understood if told.

While she remained in bed, it was our responsibility to cook, clean and do most of her work. Our first chore was washing clothes, which was a challenge because we did not have a washing machine. We used a washboard – the only thing available.

We filled the washtub with water as hot as our hands could stand. Then we scrubbed the clothes up and down on the washboard until they were clean. Once the clothes were clean, we had to place them in another tub with cool water for the rinse and wring them by hand as dry as we could.

Looking back on this era, I do not know how we did it but as the three oldest, I and my brothers, Maurice and Andrew, did the chores and prepared the meals following verbal instructions from our mother who could not function except from her bed. Of course we made mistakes and some of the food was tasteless but we survived and that is what life is all about. I learned how to make biscuits from scratch and at that time they seemed good.

One meal my mother frequently made before she became ill was cornmeal mush boiled in a kettle on the woodstove. Later, after the mush cooled, she sliced it with a knife and browned the slices on both sides in an iron pan on the stove, making a wholesome and tasty meal for us. While she was ill, we made the mush, which became a staple food for the family.

My mother and grandmother had another use for dry cornmeal, to brush it through their hair as a way to wash it. Apparently this took out all of the oil and dirt. There was no lather and they did not use water.

It was about this time that we learned of powdered milk and some bakery items, including bread, which could be purchased at the local grocery store. Those who could get permission from the city administration were allowed to buy these items for a small price. Vinton was a very small town and everyone knew each other's circumstances.

Most of the bread used in our household was homemade, baked on the wood-burning cook stove. Homemade bread was cheaper and the taste was better. I remember mixing the dough, following my mother's verbal instructions. Making homemade bread was fun for us. It took a long time for the dough to rise and then we prepared the baking pans and placed them in the oven to bake.

My father, who was still working at the time, hired a black woman to come by and help with the cooking and cleaning. I believe her name was Mrs. Butt. We looked forward to her coming. She was kind, treated us as if we were her own children and required that we do what she said without argument.

I remember her as jolly and a little heavy. She wore cloth aprons and would give us each a huge hard squeeze of a hug each time she came. At the same time, she did not allow any nonsense from any of the children. Maybe that's why we loved her. I don't know where she lived, nor do I recall any other name for her. Since I was young, my high opinion of her came from the fact that she made it a point to keep us fed and in warm clothing.

Although this was prior to my father losing his job because of the Depression, I recall that money was really tight even at that time. I knew that because rather than receiving material things from our parents, we received their love and attention.

About twenty-five black families lived only a block away from us. Mrs. Butt may have lived in one of these houses. Some of these people came by our house asking for food once the Depression set in solidly but I do not recall Mrs. Butt ever coming to seek food or assistance.

Following the fire, we lived with our grandparents and their adult children including two sons and one daughter who were deaf mutes. We were welcomed because we were family and had no other place to go. My brothers and sisters were supportive, and together we tried to enjoy life with all of its perils, hardships of hunger and deprivation and the brave fight against every person who attempted to cause the family problems. Because of our situation and our suspicion that an arsonist caused the fire, we felt like outcasts, as if others didn't care whether we lived or died.

This included the family members on my mother's side who offered very little assistance during our times of need, especially during the Depression. We did not get to know many of our family members from my father's side, so we cannot fault them as much. I do remember that my father's brother, who lived about thirty miles from us, had a Model-A Ford and visited us maybe once a year. But as a rule there was very little visiting with my father's family, mainly due to lack of funds and no transportation. Most generally we walked to places we wanted to visit.

The situation at my grandparents' house with our aunts and uncles was tense but never erupted into name-calling or other kinds of arguments because my grandparents would not allow this type of behavior. Our aunts and uncles would not allow us to take charge of anything in the house or the grounds including the garden plot that my grandfather worked on weekends. He required all of his children and grandchildren to work when he needed assistance in the garden or around the house, but always under his supervision.

At this time we learned the rule that children could be seen but not heard. There were many times we received spankings for making too much noise when grown-ups were talking.

Later as the years passed, we did many chores for our grandparents and helped them in any way possible when they began to get older and unable to work for themselves, travel or visit doctors.

Our grandmother's generosity helped us and others. When her son had an accident on the railroad, she baked cakes and took them to the hospital for the doctors, not for her son. She believed this was one of the best ways to repay the debt and recognize the doctor for his expertise. Because her son was hurt on the job, the railroad company paid all of his medical expenses.

At the same time, she recognized that her son and his family needed additional bed clothing for the coming winter. Our family needed the same.

We learned how to help in this venture by making quilts. My grandmother used a quilting frame set up in her living room. At a specific time, the family gathered and began to make quilts. Family members sewed pieces of cloth together to make squares or other shapes. These pieces were then sewn on the large piece of cloth that had been attached to the frame.

This process continued until we had a blanket large enough to fit a bed. I remember crawling under the huge frame and pulling the needle through the cloth and pushing it back so that the older people would not have to get on their hands and knees to complete this part of the job. It took several tries to put the needle in the right place. I would much rather have been outside playing. The quilts made at my grandmother's house were nice and warm. When we moved back into our partially-constructed house, we took some of them with us.

At that time, blankets had to be much larger than the bed because my grandmother had large down mattresses that made the bed high from the floor and very bulky. These beds were difficult to get into but once we became nestled within the mattress, we were very comfortable for the entire night.

To make a mattress, we had to pick the down feathers from the chickens, wash them in hot water, dry them in the sun or oven and then stuff them into a cloth with an opening on one end. Many families gathered at our grandparents' house – especially family members on my mother's side – to make mattresses and quilts for all to enjoy. At that time, many adults went to their neighbors' homes to help with chores such as making bedding, canning foods or doing other tasks.

While we were staying with my grandparents, we learned how to make soap. This happened at hog-killing time. To prepare the soap, all of the fat from the hogs was cut away and placed into an iron kettle with very little water but lots of lye, which cut the grease into particles. The entire kettle was heated for many hours over a wood-burning fire. After the boiling and stirring, the contents were allowed to cool overnight.

Generally, the soap was then cut with a knife while still in the iron kettle. The blocks of soap were placed on brown paper to harden. We used these not only for washing our faces and hands but also for washing clothes on the washboard. Every family member used this soap and I must admit it took off the dirt and grime.

My grandparents had a parlor that was off-limits to all children. We were forbidden to touch the expensive chairs and player piano without permission. To play this piano, a roll of music was inserted into an opening. Then we pumped the foot pedals to get the sound to spring forth as the roll turned. The keys would work up and down as the music played. It became a treat for us to make music on this piano.

My grandparents also had a windup victrola, which stood about four feet high. We enjoyed winding it tightly and placing the records under the needle to hear the sound. As I recall these records were 78s because there were no 33s or 45s at that time. Some of the recordings were of country music. Others consisted of talking rather than singing.

These recordings were the only type of entertainment we had; otherwise we would have had to manufacture our own pleasures or sit still in a chair. We never interrupted when adults were talking. If any child spoke up without asking to speak he or she was struck sharply on the behind and told in no uncertain terms to remain quiet.

While we were at our grandparents, we received some wearing apparel from neighbors and others – a great gift which served quite nicely. They were not usually our size but after cutting or adding to them we made out fairly well. Baggy pants and oversized sweaters and shoes were the order of the day and we stayed warm during the winter months.

We were quite conscious of the lack of suitable wearing apparel but this in no way deterred us from our beliefs that we could someday get something better. It amuses me to see young people today wearing oversized clothing, baggy trousers with gaping holes and patches who consider themselves to be well dressed.

I recall my mother sewing large patches on the knees of our overalls, as they were called at that time. We were glad to have the covering over our legs and knees even if they were patched.

Many who could afford proper clothing made remarks about the huge patches on our clothing. This made me more determined than ever to get ahead and earn things for the family and me. I learned that when a person is down with nothing to spend on himself, he will become a better person in the long run because his mental outlook changes to what he can do rather than crying over what he cannot do.

No programs or agencies provided assistance for needy families as they do today. Most of the families would not have gone to any agency anyway because of their pride and willingness to work to earn funds for themselves and their family. Our family was in that category, depending upon ourselves exclusively.

Additionally, most other families in town were in the same condition that we were. It was understood that families would help each other as best they could. At that time, this was a precept of the American way of living – doing things for ourselves and avoiding government at any level.

The Second Wiseman

Buying and Keeping Food

We all shared food and clothing when it was available. Skin color was never the criteria. The main thing to remember was that the person was a human being and in need. Therefore, all persons were helped as the situation arose. I recall that many persons who were considered hoboes from the railroad trains were thought of as vagrants. But if they wanted food, they came to our house and my mother took the time to prepare them a meal except when she was ill. She also informed them that she only had mush, corn cakes or beans, but they appreciated the food they received.

During the 1930s after a hard day's work, there was nothing more satisfying than having hot cornmeal. The corn was heated in a kettle and served on a plate with butter or salt and water to drink. I enjoyed this supper many times as a young person.

As the Depression became more severe and times became wretched, we began to worry about food and where we could get help. Sometimes we were lucky enough to get rides to an orchard where we picked apples, peaches and plums. We needed rides because we could not carry the heavy baskets the many miles back to our house. These items of food were also shared with those who asked for something to eat.

I recall that we had two or three kinds of cherry trees growing behind the house near the alleyway. One kind was the wax cherry; another was the small red cherry, both of which we shared with our neighbors, friends and family.

As children, we spent many springtime hours climbing the trees and picking the cherries for our family's consumption. We prepared them by taking out the seeds. Then our mother canned them. Our job was to ensure that they did not burn on the cooking stove. After they were canned, we stored them with the other food in the fruit house. We picked and ate cherries almost every day while they were ripe. This may be reason I am not fond of cherries today.

We also picked many bushels of apples and peaches to preserve for winter food. My father made arrangements with a local farmer who allowed us to pick the fruit from certain trees.

Apple butter was a favorite and we spent many hours washing, peeling and slicing the apples on the day before the cooking.

A copper kettle was washed prior to cooking the fruit over a wood fire. I do not recall who owned this kettle, but many families in town used the same apple-butter kettle, which was transferred from house to house during the fall.

The apples cooked in the kettle for about an hour to become soft and ready for stirring. We stirred them with a clean, wooden L-shaped paddle with a long handle. As the apples softened in the hot kettle, stirring became easier.

Making the apple butter took all day and most of the next night. After cooking, the apple butter was placed in gallon crockery containers, which had to be washed and prepared. Then they had to be covered to keep out mice or any substance that would destroy the taste.

The crockery containers were placed in the fruit house, a darkened room kept safe from vandals with an iron bar placed on the inside of the door. The only way to get the bar out was to enter the fruit house through the coal shed. We were sworn to secrecy about the iron bar and to my knowledge no one outside the family knew of it.

When it came time to can peaches, we all helped peel and seed them so that the fruit could be cooked in containers on top of the wood-burning stove. It was the duty of the children to gather the firewood. Naturally we were given instructions as to where to go and what to get because we did not know the difference in wood. We also had to heat water and clean the glass jars that held the peaches.

We placed the peaches in the jars with the tops screwed down tight. Then we placed the jars in a metal container of water, which was brought to a boil on top of the wood-fired stove.

The cooking required about six hours or more. I always wondered what kept the glass from cracking and the contents from spilling out into the water. Later I learned that the heat inside the glass rose with the heat on the outside. Maintaining equal pressure kept the glass intact.

There were no refrigerators or freezers in those days. Even if they were on the market, no one could afford to buy them. However my mother was able to secure a used icebox to assist her in keeping food fresh.

The icebox was lined with metal to hold ten and twenty-five-pound blocks of ice that sold for ten or twenty cents. The metal lining had drainage holes, which also caused the ice to melt faster. Pans placed under the icebox to catch the melt had to be emptied at least once a day or the water would overflow.

Our icebox would accommodate the ten-pound block, which is what we bought when we had the funds. For us youngsters, watching the iceman deliver ice was a thrill. He arrived on a horse-drawn wagon. A heavy cloth covered the ice in the wagon to help keep the blocks from melting. We learned that the best way to keep the ice from melting too fast in the icebox was to put sawdust over the entire block and use paper or cloth to cover it. It was messy but it kept items cold enough to prevent spoiling.

Another method was to place paper bags around the ice. Plastic was not available – it hadn't even been invented at that time.

In our house purchasing food was a strategic affair and an ongoing struggle because of spoilage and lack of money. It had to be done with precision. Our mother, who knew what was available and how much it would cost, exercised a delicate balance. Since we had little funds, there was an ongoing discussion of what to buy. We bought most of the food items for cooking on the stovetop; therefore they were the normal food staples found in most households with plenty of cornmeal and oats.

Eventually, our grandmother bought a refrigerator that was a sight to see. It had a huge round motor on the top. It took three men to place it in the kitchen. Under constant threats, we learned not to open it; nor were we permitted to take anything from the inside.

Gathering Firewood

We used wood and a very little coal to heat in the wintertime. As it was, without the proper clothing to wear or the proper bed clothing to use for warmth, we were pretty cold day and night. I recall getting out of bed in the morning in extreme cold and running downstairs to get near the stoves.

We did not at this time have a bathroom inside the house so we had to go around the building to a former toilet still standing in part of the old burned-out house. We used this toilet for a number of years and became accustomed to going outside in all kinds of weather; however we could never acclimate ourselves to these primitive conditions and extremely cold weather.

When it was raining or snowing, we were in an awkward condition. Particularly in freezing weather, we were forced to use separate containers inside the house, then empty them when we could get outside. Although this was a crude way to live, there was no other way for the family to maintain any kind of decency.

Young boys, especially in our family, had the chore to go out and find wood for heating and cooking. We obtained a crosscut saw from a family that had no need for it, and after cutting our fingers a few times, we learned how to use it. From then on we were very careful with the saw. Later, we learned to sharpen it with a file. We also obtained a sledgehammer and a chisel, which we used to split the wooden blocks. This is not an easy job.

The person holding the chisel may very well get his hand broken or bruised. But we did it and received compliments on a job well done from our parents and neighbors.

Eventually we borrowed an ax and also secured a wedge made by a neighbor, but we did not know how to use these until we got a demonstration from an elderly man and subsequently from our father. We were warned not to use the ax to strike the wedge because it would splinter the steel in the head of the ax and make it unusable.

One of our neighbors had a makeshift blacksmith shop in his garage with a forge in which he burned coke to heat the pieces of iron to make wedges for us. He heated the metal red-hot, and then shaped it with blows from a hammer, continuing this process until it formed a proper width. Then he placed it in water to temper the metal for hardness. As I recall, one of his wedges cost us twenty cents, but we used it for many years until it finally rusted to such a degree that we were forced to discard it.

Once, we heard about a group of men working on the railroad removing crossties that had deteriorated and needed replacing. We asked the foreman if we could have some of the crossties to cut and burn in our stoves for heat. He agreed to let us have about two-dozen but warned us not to get in the way of his men or any oncoming trains.

We had to move these crossties from the embankment where his men had thrown them. These crossties had a lot of fiber left in them for using in a wood stove. We used this wood to keep us in heat for almost an entire winter even though it contained creosote as a preservative.

Maurice, Andrew, and I made a sawhorse from old lumber pieces to hold the crossties between the uprights. Then we learned that we could saw them into small pieces at specified lengths that could fit nicely into the cook stove without their needing to be split. We measured and cut a piece of wood to be used as a template for the kitchen stove, then we used the same method to cut pieces for the heater in the family room adjacent to the kitchen, furnishing pleasant heat for the family.

None of these things went off without some arguing among us as to how to best complete the job. Many times we engaged in fights with each other over the work, playing baseball or other activities. When that happened, our parents had to break up the fight and direct us in how to complete the work or continue to play peacefully.

We learned that there are many ways to complete a job but we did not know the exact way. After a few fists flew, we finally devised a method for hauling the crossties home. We used a homemade wagon that one of us pulled by a rope while the other two pushed from the side and rear. Picturing it in my mind today, I have to chuckle about how that started.

We began with a basic idea of a bed for the wagon and added a tongue and mismatched wheels, which we collected from trash cans. Then we added boards to the side so smaller things we'd be hauling wouldn't fall out. It wasn't anything like a factory-made wagon but it worked and that's what counted.

Over the next few years, we used our wagon for many things but generally it was for hauling firewood for the cook stove and the heater. We hoped that the warmth would heat that room and penetrate the ceiling to the upstairs bedrooms.

Although some of our neighbors and friends asked us to gather firewood for them, we declined because we did not have the time or the implements to carry out the work and did not know how to go into business for ourselves. We only worked for our family and under the instructions of our parents.

As mentioned previously, most cooking was accomplished on wood-burning stoves and the wood had to be cut and stored where it would be dry. Some households used coal but in addition to our lack of storage space, it was too expensive for us. Generally, a basement held stored coal. Dust and soot filled the air and covered everyone who came in contact with coal. When the coal became wet, it was difficult to get a fire started unless small pieces of wood were first used to start the fire.

Our neighbor had an unused driveway and we had permission to have the coal truck back up to a small shed and unload any coal we could buy. Since coal and wood were the main source of energy, every home most generally used the coal to heat as well as cook food on the stoves. These could make the house very hot in the summer time; however the heat it produced during the winter months proved to be most enjoyable.

School Days

Everyone knew you had to be six years old before the end of September to enroll in school for that school year. There were no exceptions. Since my birthday was in November, I had to wait until the following year to attend school. This set me back one year in my studies, which I regret even to this day.

During the early 1930s and 40s there were no preschool programs and no kindergarten. We learned from our peers, parents or relatives but this was not considered home schooling by any means.

Our grade school, now named the Cook Elementary School, was just a few blocks from my grandparents' home. Our strict teachers made learning easy because we received generous doses of ruler learning on the hands and on the rear when we did not know the lessons. I remember one teacher who appeared to be old and weak physically but very demanding when she gave us lessons. She did not accept any talking, laughing or other childlike input in her classroom. She taught first grade through fifth grade students in one room.

At the time, school scared me but today that time seems like the most enjoyable of my life. We learned many topics and many social mores, including manners and discipline. Above all we learned about God and religion. We began each day with a prayer and the Pledge of Allegiance.

We learned many things about World War I and the hardships encountered by the soldiers who went to France. This was my first real insight into army life, taught by someone who had not served in the military. We were fortunate in having such a fine teacher and I consider myself blessed having had dedicated teachers in every class. These teachers spoke plainly and truthfully to all students and had answers for all of our questions. They taught us with stern discipline, strictly enforced.

When I entered high school, I recall another teacher – a grand lady who was quite instrumental in my education. Her actions and her words carried us through the grades without many mishaps because she demanded that we learn the topics under discussion. I appreciate this teacher, whom my wife and I got to know socially later in life as a very fine and gracious person. She, as well as our other teachers introduced pride in our thinking and actions toward others and insisted on discipline and knowledge.

It was during these times that my two brothers and I were given the name "The Three Wise Men." I do not remember where it originated but the students used that term in referring to us. We did not resent any names they called us unless the names implied that we were lower in status than they. All boys in our family had a middle name that started with a W. My middle name is Walter.

We continued to live at our grandparents' house for a number of years until, near the time of our leaving grammar school, we moved into the partially-built house. Then we went to junior high school, a few miles further away than grammar school but we still walked to get there. After two years in junior high, we entered William Byrd High School.

Because the teachers ensured that the topics were informative and above all important to our future, school was not tiring, nor was it a chore to attend. We learned, recited and wrote by practice and more practice. Most of the teachers loved their work and created interesting projects for us to do.

Because we feared the teachers, most of the students, including me, completed our assignments on time and in the correct manner. Most children's parents had not completed grammar school. Some had not gone past fourth grade.

Sometimes children's chores took precedence over studies, which set most of us back in our school grades. These chores included earning money for food and clothing, cleaning the house and surrounding areas and running errands.

William Byrd High School was about four miles from our house if we took the short cut through a farmer's field. If we walked around the field, it was more than five miles. There were many social functions at school, generally occurring in the fall of the year. Usually though, there was a five- or ten-cent admission fee to defray the cost of the function, so pleasurable as it sounded to be able to attend, we rarely could afford to.

I can never express in words how much I appreciated having a coat or jacket in the rain or snow because we walked to school in all weather. There were no buses to pick us up. The buses were only available for the students who lived in the county at least twenty miles from the school. They ran intermittently, especially if the snow was very deep and the roads were not passable, as frequently happened in the winter months. If the buses were late, the children came to classes when they arrived at the school. I do not recall that the schools were closed due to snow as they are in the present.

Frequently teachers asked me to drive one of their cars to the city to pick up items for them. I learned that they trusted me and I felt obligated to dignify that trust by conducting myself in a proper manner. I never had an accident with their automobiles. Speeding was the farthest thing from my mind because I did not want them to think badly of me.

The teachers were well qualified to teach different topics and they were open and above-board to all students. We were disciplined and taught to believe that we could get along with each other. It was not unusual for the teachers to paddle our hands when we did something wrong and I must say this was more embarrassing than painful because our peers watched the procedure. Consequently, we attempted to avoid getting caught doing anything that would cause us embarrassment in the presence of other students.

Employment During the Depression

This small town of Vinton, with a population of less than two thousand, is categorized as rural. Most everyone in the town knew each other, affording close relationships among our neighbors and friends. This became important when the Depression hit all of the families extremely hard. There were limited materials as well as opportunities. But there were no crimes that we knew about. We heard of thievery on a small scale, but nothing to become excited over in such a small town.

Since everybody knew each other, most of the young persons would not dare commit any offenses for fear of being identified and punished. This punishment could be right on the spot by the nearest adult but then another punishment was in order when the culprit arrived home. There was no getting around it. There were no secrets. Everybody knew what we did, including our parents, before we arrived home. I have no explanation for how this news traveled at such a speed but it did and our parents knew exactly what we did and how we accomplished the feat.

When I speak of punishment I do not mean a stern talking to nor screaming at the offender. I mean a spanking from the nearest adult, who generally used his hand to strike us on the behind a number of times while admonishing us not to repeat the offense again. By this method we young persons learned what to do and what not to do because the resulting spanking would reinforce our thinking. The offense was not repeated, at least in the presence of adults.

Because of the stern discipline and guidance we all received when we were young and eager, I believe that as members of the armed forces in later years we were able to endure the hardships and complete the war. The only recourse available to any family was to correct their children, ensuring that they would learn from the corrective action taken by neighbors and family friends. There were no consultants, psychologists, sociologists or social engineers to intervene and set everything right for all persons. The family controlled the offspring, usually with the assistance of neighbors and friends. This protective system, it is safe to assume, was the forerunner of neighborhood-watch organizations.

Looking back at this aspect of my own personal experience, I am ever so thankful that there were no specialists involved in raising us. In my opinion, the small amount of pain we received from our parents and neighbors as a result of spankings made us better people. I am not advocating that children be abused but that they encounter sufficient pain that they will remember the lesson.

In addition, the embarrassment would normally suffice especially if their peers observed the process. They in turn, would tease the culprit for getting caught, causing an additional embarrassment as well as a bitter pill to swallow for children under twelve. Most of us remember how we would try to get away with petty things and gloat to our peers how we survived the time and the incident, especially how we put one over on our parents or neighbors.

As time moved slowly forward, we emerged into the 1930s, a time described by many who lived through it as a painful, wretched era of absolutely no food and very few fond memories. We must never forget the '30s because this great country almost became lost. The people suffered the most horrible hunger pangs, wanting not only for food but adequate clothing and shelter and heat during the winter months.

There was little or no work for anyone. In fact there was more unemployment than most people, especially politicians, wanted to admit and most of those employed were getting very low wages. Back then there was no minimum wage. Most men worked for twenty-five or fifty cents per day – per day, not per hour. Some did not even earn that much.

At that time hourly work was computed from sunup to sundown depending upon the employer's available funds, not by hours on the clock. Work usually began at five in the morning and ended after the sun had set. Once daylight was gone, unless kerosene lamps or candles were available, people learned to suffer through the pangs of getting food to eat in the dark.

The working time was important to all who were interested in earning money. During the summer, the day could begin even earlier. There was no daylight saving time – only early in the morning before the sun rose could we say that we were saving time.

Everyone worked seven days a week. Very few took time off for anything, even to go to church on Sunday, because food was a must and the family had to be fed daily. I was too young to recall a lot of things except hunger during those early days of the Depression when everyone was just trying to stay alive.

Long lines of people waited to get a job, any job, wherever one was available. The word "sweatshop" was never mentioned. The workers would not use this word as a way of getting back at the employer because employment was money and everyone needed money to live.

The politicians came around the town center and talked a great deal, hoping that someone would vote for them. They did not know the answers, just like today, but they expounded on and on without saying anything important. There were few unions, and if one started, the workers would run them out of town or off the workplace just to maintain their work habits and especially to maintain their salaries. It was a foregone conclusion that the workers would never say anything against their employer because it meant they would be fired on the spot and would have nowhere to turn for employment.

When we were working for a local farmer, we had to be in the field at sunrise to cut corn and do other farm work. We used our own knives to cut the dried corn stalks after the corn had been harvested. I used to think there would never be an end to those rows. I still have the same knife I used then. It has a long machete blade, with many nicks where I innocently struck rocks and other objects while doing a day's work.

Some of the young boys obtained jobs carrying out groceries at one of the stores, but this was day-to-day employment. Others attempted to find work from neighbors. If they were lucky, they received about five cents a day.

I recall an open ore mine being worked near the town limits close to the cemetery. Fortunately my father got a job as a truck driver at this mine when it opened because he knew the foreman. After he was hired, he took us to see the operation. It was awesome to me as a young boy.

The truck my father drove was not the type seen today. It had large wheels with solid rubber tires. The first time I rode in it, I almost bounced out of the seat because the wheels met the roadway with such force. The seat was hard and small and just my size. There were huge chains on the engine, which were attached to sprockets on both rear wheels. With its heavy load of iron ore, it operated very slowly.

The truck bed was chained down so when the operator was ready to unload the ore, the chain had to be disconnected from the side. The bed turned in every way except forward, to prevent the load from crushing the cab and driver.

At this time, no cranes existed to lift the stones and iron ore. All of this had to be accomplished by manpower, using shovels and makeshift runways from the top of the pile to where the ore was dumped into the truck. Many times the large rocks required two or more men to roll them.

In most cases dynamite was used to explode large rocks into smaller pieces of stone that one person could handle. The dynamite was inserted into a hole drilled into the rock. One person would hold a star drill to the rock while another would strike the drill with a sledgehammer. After each strike, the drill would be turned slightly and in this fashion a hole would be driven into the stone.

The ore was deposited in a wooden chute, where it traveled a short distance to a huge iron jaw that crushed it into very small pieces. These pieces were then loaded into a rail car sitting on a siding of the railroad tracks. When the car was filled, the owner of the mine called the railroad to come get it and an engine hauled it away to the train station for transportation to a smelting factory.

The truck my father drove had little protection. In fact it had no roof, doors, window glass or windshield because large rocks might fall on it at any time and crush or shatter these truck parts. But that also meant that nothing protected the driver from sun or falling rocks, which came from the dynamiting that separated the iron ore from the rocks in the ground.

From my grandparents' home I could watch this truck going back and forth from the open ore mines to the railroad tracks about five miles away. The narrow roads of dirt, sand and rock, with holes and ruts made from runoff water, made driving difficult.

After about a year, the mine closed because it became unproductive to mine the iron ore. Then my father and the others lost their jobs.

Sometime during the early 1930s a neighbor, Carroll Dooley, who was in France during World War I, discussed his idea of marching on Washington, D.C. to obtain a pension for the war veterans. At the time, I had no earthly idea why he felt this way. Washington was on another planet as far as I was concerned. But later, my own experiences took a turn in this same direction. Mr. Dooley was 1st Sergeant in an Army unit training in Vinton and his son, Carroll Junior, was a family friend. In the late '30s, I worked for Mr. Dooley in the roofing business.

Some of the young fellows my age sought work as delivery carriers for *The Roanoke Times*, the local newspaper. Most of the news was about the depression and the lack of funds for families to survive.

These delivery routes were difficult to get because everyone who was seeking employment was ready, willing and able to take over when there was a vacancy, regardless of the location. Newspapers sold for three cents each. Paper carriers could make around fifteen cents each week, not counting the occasional penny tips. I considered myself very fortunate because I was able to obtain my own newspaper delivery route.

I recall one customer who became very angry when I failed to place his newspaper under the porch rug a certain way, according to his instructions. This customer finally paid me after I returned to his house a second time for collection. Eventually his payment included a penny tip.

Generally speaking, everyone was looking for work and would do most anything short of crime to get any job available. As indicated earlier, most of the work was on farms, cutting corn, storing silage and moving equipment from one place to another. Because of the keen competition, younger persons got the jobs because they could work faster for less pay.

Many horse-drawn wagons and later, trucks went to the surrounding farms daily to pick up filled milk cans. They left empty containers for the farmers to fill with milk and have ready the following day. One milk route was fairly close to where I lived, but I was too young to get a job as a driver. I would have to depend on an older person who could drive to hire me as a worker.

But most of the drivers would not hire a young boy of ten or eleven because he might get hurt and the driver did not have the funds to pay medical bills. This was explained to every person who was hired for work at any job, regardless of his age. Back then there was no insurance to help an employee and an employer could not afford to hire someone who might get hurt.

Once I heard of a driver who needed a delivery boy to help deliver milk. He was expected to run from the delivery truck and back in just a minute or less. This work began at four a.m. and did not end until about ten a.m. the same day.

When I learned about this position, I spent one whole morning searching before I found the truck driver to ask him for the job, which I got. This work was only on Saturday and Sunday mornings. The driver paid for my breakfast and also paid me a dollar from his pocket along with a quart of milk to take home for the other members of the family.

Although I have forgotten the name of the driver, my family and I appreciated his actions because we did not have the money to buy milk. I had no hesitancy in telling him that we did not have the funds for most things that others may have taken for granted.

This man offered and I accepted his guidance on many things. In my opinion, he was a God-fearing man who had a family to support. He was not about to jeopardize his employment by doing anything illegal or not called for by his employer, the Clover Creamery Company, located in the southeast section of Roanoke. This company sold milk-related products for many years. Most farmers delivered their products daily to this creamery.

There were no racial problems that I could recall at any of the workplaces. We all were told of the sign placed in the center of town by an unknown person, which allegedly said, "Nigger, don't let the sun set on you in this town." However, we lived within a block of a number of black families and there was never any problem.

I do remember one curious incident when I was in the employ of a local farmer. It happened on a Saturday around noon, when we all got paid. I did not approve of it, but I could not voice my opinion because I was too young to understand its significance. Also I was afraid I might be fired if I said anything.

There was an elderly black man who worked for the farmer on a full-time basis. When he was given some money, the farmer stated, "You don't need all that money. Here. I will give you this much."

I do not recall the exact amount but it was several dollars less than the worker had earned for the entire week. I am sure this elderly man needed the money just as badly as any of us and could have kept his family in a better way than they were living.

I must admit that some black families lived in better homes than we had and they may have had more to eat. I know that they had funds to buy coal to heat their houses because we saw the smoke rising from their chimneys and the coal piles in the yards near their houses.

Shopping and Values

We learned to save everything. Today we would call this recycling, but back then we saved things because we might need it tomorrow and no person knew what the next day would bring. If we did not use or need the article, there was always someone who could; this is what was meant by being helpful and using all our resources frugally.

We carried a bucket or shopping bag with us everywhere because we never knew what kind of food items or other things we would have to carry home. There were no shopping centers then and no specific items we could always count on buying because generally we had no funds. We would barter or beg for food items whenever they could be found. We took care never to lose these items because this might mean the difference between life and death. We became quite frugal at an early age – a habit that remains with us to this day.

Sometimes we heard about stealing from stores or other places, mostly involving food items for families. In our family stealing was an offense that would cause us to get a spanking. It was not considered a heinous crime to get food for a starving child. However we were taught to ask for anything we needed and warned never to steal. Adults took special care to provide food and clothing for children and others in need. After all, the children remained the future of this great country regardless of the time of year or the condition under which we all lived.

We children often enjoyed walking to go to a movie – a rare treat because of the expense. However, we could stay all day at that time. This would include the cartoons that most of us enjoyed more than the movies. But Tom Mix and Ken Maynard or any cowboy for that matter was a hero to all of us. Many of the movies were serials, with installments every week for many weeks. We knew this was a way to get more patrons to come to the movies even at the exorbitant price of ten cents. Very few had the five-cent streetcar fare to Roanoke about ten miles away. Most of us young people walked the distance without grumbling, especially to go the movies.

In order to earn money for these expenses, we would hunt for iron, copper and brass pieces to sell for cash at a junkyard located on the way to the movies. Each of us would carefully count the pennies because this was the only way we could have an afternoon of enjoyment. If any money was left over we spent it on a hot dog and a coke, which cost another five cents each. We could only go to the movies about once a month because it took that long to gather the pieces of iron and other salable items to earn money for the admission.

We walked to Roanoke when we needed to make special purchases. One of the places we'd go was the market where all farmers brought their produce to sell. This market had dry-goods stores along with other outlets. The Norfolk and Western Railroad Headquarters was about one block from the farmers' market, and the railroad repair shops encompassed many blocks.

My grandfather worked as a carpenter for the railroad company, now called Norfolk Southern. For his entire working life, he walked fifteen miles to work each day from his home in Vinton. He repaired the caboose and other wooden parts of the train.

Once in his later life, he told about the time he owed a man fifty cents, which he had borrowed for a final payment on a debt. But on payday, the man was not around. He lived about twenty-five miles east of Vinton. My grandfather walked there and back just to pay back his debt to that man. This type of honesty impressed my young mind.

My grandfather was a God-fearing man who never missed a day reading the Bible and to my knowledge he never used profane language when he spoke. Everyone who knew my grandfather had the utmost respect for him. His word was his bond.

My grandfather believed that it would be best never to owe money to any person at any time and he tried to live true to this belief. He impressed the idea on me that if I owed any person, I then would be obligated to him until the debt was paid. He also told me that in between the payments of the debt I would be obligated to abide by what the man said and I would be under that man's dictates for as long as I owed him money.

My grandfather informed me that it required three years and three months to read the Bible, one chapter each day. I tested this and sure enough, it took that much time to read the Bible from cover to cover. Even after this exercise I did not understand all that I had read at that time in my young life.

Rebuilding the House

Around 1935 a logger offered my father timber in exchange for his assistance cutting down trees and sawing them into boards for building. As part of the exchange, we boys would have to help when they needed us. When the time came, we rode about twenty miles to the top of the mountain where the men were working and learned how it was done.

First, the trees were cut down with an ax and a crosscut saw. Then chains were tied around the trees and attached to the collars of a team of mules.

The animals pulled the logs to the saw frames where men loosened the chains and rolled the logs over to be cut. The tree was placed securely into a slot on the wooden frames. Then the mules pulled it against the fast running blade of the saw.

The tree was turned over and sawed many times at each turn. The supporting frame holding the log allowed the operator to cut the log to a predetermined size. My father operated the saw many times while we were with him at the mountain and he used us for many jobs as he saw the need.

A gasoline engine attached to the rear wheel of an old automobile operated the saw blade by a belt connected to this wheel. The speed of the engine made the saw blade run fast. A high frame around the saw blade was the only safety measure to keep people from walking into the blade. This was not an effective safety device although I never saw anyone get hurt.

We worked for many days during the summer months loading and unloading two-by-four, two-by-six, two-by-eight and some four-by-four boards. We finally got enough lumber, even though it was rough-cut, to begin the construction on our house.

But before we could begin the rebuilding we had to haul away the burned-out portions of the old house to make room for the new building. Then we dug ditches and made forms to pour concrete into the ground for a footing. In building the forms we carefully secured them to each other to prevent the heavy weight of the concrete from seeping or running out of the openings. To do this we placed iron pieces, solid rock and other similar articles against the forms to help hold the weight. We did everything by hand including making the mixer box with wooden boards.

That old homemade wagon we used to haul firewood served us well. With it we hauled in sand and gravel and most of the heavy items. Every week or two we collected sand from a branch in the stream that ran beside the railroad tracks in front of the house. Our father showed us how to make a hole in the bank of the stream to collect it. Then we shoveled the sand into the wagon and hauled it to the place where we would later mix it with gravel and cement.

The gravel was purchased from a quarry over a period of time when money was available. Meanwhile, we kept gathering the sand until we had a very large pile.

Finally, my father had enough money to buy a few bags of cement. Then we started to rebuild our house from the ground up. It took two of us to lift these hundred-pound bags. Many days we mixed concrete in the homemade wooden box for at least eight hours, especially on Saturday. No wheelbarrow was available so we moved the wooden mixer box close to the place where we shoveled out the cement.

Finally, the footing and some of the walls were completed. From there we began building four rooms where the family could live. During some of this rebuilding, two men helped my father. They claimed to be carpenters but their accomplishments failed to meet their claims. Several years after they completed their work, the entire end of the house began to pull away from the framing because it was not secured.

When that happened, my brothers and I climbed into the attic with our father and nailed supporting timbers to the existing framing. By starting on one end and using two-by-fours, we secured the end to the middle of the attic. This should have been done when the building was under construction.

My father told me that these men worked part-time because he did not have the money to pay their wages, which at that time were high. From my perspective, they lacked the necessary skills to build a house.

Nevertheless, two rooms were begun on the lower level and two rooms were planned on the upper level. The workers complained about the green lumber my father brought in on a borrowed truck, saying the size and thickness was not proper to complete the job correctly. However after seeing the wall pulling away from the other portion of the house, I had no sympathy for either of them.

These four rooms would not pass inspection by today's standards or be approved by building codes especially when there would be six children and two adults living in our house. But we were inside a building and out of the raw weather even though it was only partially built with no insulation.

During the winter months the cold wind sounded like a teakettle on a hot stove, with the whistle dying down as the fire cools. Even today when a teakettle begins to whistle I remember those cold damp days when the wind literally blew through the sides of the house, making everyone uncomfortable and cold.

Since we did not have a hot-water heater, on Saturday night we heated water on the top of the cook stove and carried it to a large washtub for our baths. There was no warmth in any of the rooms except the kitchen where the wood stove kept us warm while heating and cooking foods.

My father persuaded a plumber to show him where to place a hot-water tank and how to hook it to the stove. This was a chore. A coiled pipe was placed in the firebox of the stove where the hot coals would heat the metal and therefore heat the water inside the pipe. One end of the pipe was attached to the water tank, which collected the hot water. Another pipe ran from the tank to the faucet.

During the summer it became terribly hot indoors, even with the windows opened. We did not have fans or air conditioners. In fact, I do not recall any of these in the entire town. We did not even have electricity. Most of the time we depended on kerosene lamps for light.

Eventually, we obtained electric lights, a fantastic and wonderful event. Our lights were strung on one wire hanging from the center of the ceiling. Even though they were not bright, they were better than the lantern that cast shadows, making it difficult to see. Then we could read books the school issued us or the ones we bought for our classes. We also had the option of renting books from the school library for a few cents a month.

About this time my father, after having had a few drinks, came home one evening with a man and a woman. He said they were married and that they would live with us for a few weeks. They seemed nice except that they did not associate with us nor did they bring in any food to eat or clothing for us to use.

After about three weeks, the local chief of police interrupted us one night, arrested them for not being married and took them to jail. After this we never heard anything about them.

I now believe that they were in a house where they sold moonshine and were forced to vacate or be charged with selling illegal liquor. It could have been the house about one block from us. Since our house had only one room for us boys to sleep in at the time, with this couple living with us we had to sleep on the floor on a pallet in order to provide room for the unmarried couple.

There were virtually no drugs or liquor openly available then. If people used them, they did so in private. Most young people knew of these activities but no one made an issue of it because a live-and-let-live attitude prevailed. A number of people or families made 'shine, as it was called, and it registered about 100-proof provided it was made correctly.

Most of the young people knew where to get this mixture but none ever dared go to these places for fear of being seen and severely admonished. I recall a small house about a block from where we lived where a man made 'shine and sold it from his house. Many times we would see the police going into the old house and then we would see the man being taken downtown to jail. The police chief had no automobile. The prisoner walked past our house on the way to the jail, prodded along in handcuffs.

The house the moonshine manufacturer lived in was somewhat hidden by trees, with a creek that ran nearby. Most generally if the creek rose from heavy rainfall, it would flood the house covering it almost to the roof.

To us kids, this was a spooky place and we were very nervous about approaching the building. I remember quite well where the small house stood because we would go to a house across the creek from there to get a haircut.

Irving Landsdown gave the haircuts. He charged ten cents, later increasing it to fifteen cents per person. We waited for many weeks to get a haircut, by which time our hair was rather long and difficult to cut. Mr. Landsdown used his back porch to cut hair because he could sweep the hair out into the back yard when he was finished.

Eventually another child increased our family to seven, making life shakier because we were barely getting along with food and clothing. It appeared to us at that time that we were heading for a dead-end street. However, our mother always offered hope and prayers to prove that we were a family, all working toward the day when things would get better and there would be a bountiful year.

Our hopes were no different than many others with identical problems. Among our hopes was our belief in God, enforced by a Christian mother who never allowed us to do things against her religious beliefs. In fact, I never heard my mother say a cruel word or curse anyone. She never voiced opposition to the unmarried people living with us that I recall. She was an angel, if there can be one on earth.

My mother always thought of the family and its importance for the future. The children of our family will always be proud of her and the way she encouraged us to excel in everything we attempted. It was she who thanked us for small things and did not compare them to what other people or families had done.

We attended the Presbyterian Church when we were not working. My mother was a non-denominational believer and went to revival meetings. She prayed to God daily. At those times we would not talk to her or ask questions. There was no argument about any person's beliefs.

My mother always instilled in us the attitude that regardless of his religion, each person had a right to follow his own course of action. We were taught never to make fun of any person, no matter what the reason, and to be honest, truthful and above all respectful of another person's age, status in life and beliefs. My mother believed every person belonged to God and it was not our decision to say or do anything that would be wrong or contrary to Him.

These things made us more respectful. Later in life, following my father's death when our mother became ill and too feeble to remain in the house alone, she attempted to convince us that she was doing just fine. But we all knew that this was her way to avoid hurting us or having us believe she was in need.

Although she managed for years to live alone, eventually we had to talk her into going into a nursing home. She was a patient in nursing homes, both in Roanoke and Vinton, for about fifteen years and we continued to love her and visit as often as possible.

Every time we visited her she mentioned what she would do when she went home. She almost knew when she would die and tried to tell us many things about her difficult life. She was a hard worker and never complained even though she was required to work long hours at home prior to her marriage to our father. In short, though our mother had a painful and arduous life, she led a God-fearing life, as she was taught.

She had only a grade-school education because at that time formal education was not considered necessary for women. Their status in life revolved around the household chores, cooking and working in the fields. In her case there was no farm, only the family chores.

During the severe Depression, government programs for hunger eventually became available to assist as many families as possible. These programs were established before the end of the 1930s because the population was starving and almost everywhere people were dying. Occasionally I collected food for the family, as directed by my parents.

During this period I accompanied my father to a grocery store in Roanoke, as we needed ground cornmeal and flour. But the store refused to give my father credit because the grocery bill he previously incurred had not been paid. At that time I was quite young and did not understand the circumstances or the reason we could not get the cornmeal and other food items we needed.

I recall the owner of the grocery store was neither polite nor kind in his words toward my father, which made me think badly of him. We had no food in the house and the cornmeal my father wanted to get was for our meals, breakfast, lunch and supper.

Now though, I understand and feel remorseful because the grocery store owner had to make ends meet by offering credit to many people. After having experience with finances of my own, I know that the credit the owner offered would go only as far as his own funds could be spread.

We bought butter from a person who came to our house once each month. At fifteen cents a pound, the price was much cheaper than the distribution center at the stores. The person who delivered it churned it on her farm. She had molds to make different shapes and on some of the molds she had cutouts to give the finished product a different look. She sold two-pound butter in a round or square design.

The Depression seemed to continue endlessly as we struggled to stay warm and dry in our partially-rebuilt home and secure the food we needed to survive. Our parents' guidance and persistence allowed us to survive these horrible years.

Fun and Play

The weather caused our family considerable stress, but at the same time we children participated in winter activities for fun during our growing years. Beginning in September, it would snow and then freeze. This type of weather remained with us until about early April of the following year. Our family could not afford a sleigh, but others would loan us theirs to ride down the hills on the snow and ice.

This ride began about two or three blocks up one of the hills on the roadway where vehicles normally ran; however there were very few vehicles. If we had a cardboard box, we used that and rode down the hill until it became so worn that it fell apart.

In our area, the only vehicular traffic would be the streetcars at the bottom of the hill, at the end of the ride. Many times daredevil young ones came close to the streetcars and it is amazing that we did not get hurt. Of course our parents did not know the danger we were involved in and most of the kids agreed it would be better not to mention it.

This we called fun and we continued to sleigh ride on the downhill runs until it became dark and we had to report to our parents for supper and maybe an explanation of our activities. Even though we might get scolded or spanked for doing something we were not supposed to be doing, we told our parents what we had been doing because sooner or later they would find out anyway.

These sleigh rides and children's games provided happy memories for me because generally, we never had the time or the opportunity to participate in games. As a matter of fact, my father did not believe in games for children and stated that we could do certain jobs around the house and yard and get our exercise in that manner.

If we were not going to school, we worked assisting family members around our home under constant instruction from our parents. We had the normal childhood arguments with each other over small things such as how to play or who to play with but we never threatened to do physical harm to our own family members.

In fact we were too scared to make threats toward any of our playmates.

There was a larger boy who played with us known as the bully of the group. He bossed others around, demanding to have his way on everything. Once he picked a fight with me. When he struck me, without thinking or saying a word, I instantly struck him in the eye with my fist. This of course ended the playing and sleigh riding and the others decided to go home. When I told my father about the incident, he cautioned me never to start a fight with my friends.

A streetcar track ran directly in front of our house about 150 feet from the property line to the center of town, about ten blocks from our house. A public road of dirt and cinders ran alongside the streetcar rails between the streetcar tracks and our house. On the other side of these rails were railroad tracks, which the railroad company used daily for their freight and passenger trains.

A block from our house, the road going west toward Roanoke crossed Glade Creek on a portion of cement laid in the water for vehicular traffic. Trestles from the railroad tracks spanned the water there as well, many times causing flooding during thunderstorms or heavy rains. The water would have no place to run so it backed up to our house and other houses in the short block from the creek.

On several occasions the water got into our house. There was nothing we could do but watch it rise while we tried to get personal belongings out of the way and go to higher ground. Then we had no place to go until the water receded. One flood rose about three feet into the second story of our house. This ruined everything including our beds and what little food we had.

Our parents warned us not to play in or around the water because raw sewage was dumped into this creek. The town council had passed no restrictions and in almost every section of town, no one thought anything of running a sewer line from the houses down to the creek. In fact, this creek bank was also used as the town dump for many years. The chief of police would catch runaway or mad dogs and take them to the dump where he shot them and left the bodies. Then he cut off the noses in order to receive pay from the county treasurer.

We young boys disobeyed all parental guidance and explored the unknown when we learned that snakes were in the creek. We wanted to find out about the snakes and whatever else roamed the waters.

Once my older brother Maurice and I observed two snakes near one of the sewer outlets. We made a pact to catch these snakes but had no place to take them. Unafraid of the water or the reptiles, I walked into the water and slowly approached the snakes. I caught one in my left hand and then another in my right hand. The snakes were about two feet long, writhing and jumping around but I held on very tightly and began running up the street toward our house with my brother running along beside me.

For that I received a harsh and blistering spanking, which I deserved. Andrew did not go with us because he was probably too small at that time. I do not recall but I may have released these snakes in a spring running under the railroad trestle across from our house.

There were frogs living in a fresh-water pond on the other side of the railroad tracks. We could hear them almost every night. My brothers and I conspired to gig them with weapons we made from nails and lengths of wood about four feet long. Using the rail track as an anvil, we beat the nails into spear shapes with a hammer. Then we drove the nails into the wood, which we used as a handle.

Following a method we learned from our friends and with the encouragement of some adults, we found a flashlight and after dark, we roamed around the pond until we spotted a frog. Most of the time we could hear them just by walking around the water's edge. The flashlight blinded the frogs and then we stabbed them. We did this to furnish food for our family. Today, many people look upon frogs' legs as a delicacy. I agree.

The pond where the frogs lived was privately owned. It had its own water supply coming from underground springs with no known pollutants. The runoff water from the pond went into Glade Creek, where I caught the snakes and where we later got sand for building the foundations of our house.

Glade Creek began at the foot of a mountain approximately fifteen miles east of our house. It ran through farms and other properties and was ideal for young boys to explore and especially to go swimming. We had a special swimming hole about halfway between our house and the mountain.

One day, two or three of us decided to go swimming in the old swimming hole. We did not get permission or tell anyone where we were going. When we finally got to the swimming hole, as we talked about our exploits, I admitted that I could not swim. The others kept joking around and finally one of the guys pushed me into the water. I remember going down over my head and a burning feeling overwhelming me.

To this day I do not recall getting pulled out of the water. The only thing I remember is coming to my senses on the bank of the creek with the guys pushing and pulling on me.

The guy who pushed me in was scared. He said he thought I could swim. He was also the one who pulled me out of the water. He said I fought him like a tiger. I must admit that I never mentioned this episode to my parents or family for fear of being punished.

Beyond the swimming hole was the mountain that we boys used to explore, especially after we joined a Boy Scout troop, the first one in Vinton. We used the mountain as a hideout and play area for many years. As scouts, we earned many badges and much gratitude from the citizens of the town for our service.

Our scoutmaster continually thought of ways to improve our self-esteem by getting us to assist in various projects whenever he could. One was to climb the mountain and blaze a trail for others to follow.

As we trudged along on that climb, we cut away branches and small trees and marked the larger trees so that we and others could follow the trail to the top. It took us about five hours to climb the mountain while carrying all the supplies we needed for two days and nights.

Once, like Tarzan, we took off our clothes and tried to outdo each other swinging on the vines. This was a mistake for as we learned later, we all got bad cases of poison ivy or poison oak, which took many weeks of home doctoring to cure. Needless to say, I did not do that stupid trick again.

We children had difficult times as we were growing up but the adults also had difficult times. Still, they were ever mindful of the needs of all children. No child was left unattended in any kind of dangerous situation. An adult would protect him until his parents or guardian came to get him. A lonely or lost child would be escorted home to safety with his or her family.

In my mind, this was the ever-present security that each child needs in everyday life. Most of us had a nothing-can-hurt-me attitude, which prevails today in our young people. We must protect, teach and discipline our children and young people because they are our future.

Sure, we got our share of licks and bumps and cuts in fights with each other, injuries detected the moment we entered the house. We had our share of rock throwing and hitting each other with sticks or whatever came into our minds at the time. But we were not vicious, nor were we trying to kill each other.

Neighborhood security depended upon each of us watching for anybody who might be considering mischief. We had a fine neighborhood watch system to live in as children, enforced by the adults' presence as well as their corrective guidance, making security uppermost in the minds of all children. To be secure was to be safe.

Our parents sternly informed us boys that there would be no fighting with girls. To strike or hit a girl – even one of our sisters – would bring sudden and severe punishment. Even to make adverse comments against our sisters in anger would bring a spanking from our father with a razor strap and a stern warning that if we did the same thing again we would get a more severe punishment. His warnings to us were sufficient and we were mortally afraid to hit or threaten our sisters in any manner.

At this time, no family locked their doors. Anyone could walk into a neighbor's house at will but this never happened because all family members in town were taught to honor the privacy of another household. All children learned this respect for others. A knock at the door or a loud call of the person's name would suffice to give notice that we wanted to enter the house of a neighbor or friend. In fact, the doors to our house were never locked until around 1949, well after World War II, and then it was not every day or night but just on an occasional basis.

Around 1938 our next-door neighbors, who were well regarded by everyone, bought an automobile. They built a garage to store it in at the end of a narrow driveway close to our house. On Sundays they drove to church or to visit their families in the town or surrounding country. The wife was the only one who learned to drive. The husband refused to learn.

We knew whenever they were getting ready to leave in their car because the wife raced the engine of the car so loud and long that we were afraid she would accidentally lose control of the clutch, making the car jump forward or backward and cause severe damage. Naturally as children we had a few private laughs about her driving and her ability to handle the car, but she never had an accident. We learned later after they moved from the neighborhood that they had to sell the car because it quit running.

These neighbors respected us, and we looked upon them as honest and dependable friends. The husband worked for the railroad company. They made life a little easier for us by dropping change on the ground for us to find from time to time.

We had no way to know for sure that they were the ones who dropped the money. But I recall one time I was digging a hole in the ground when my mother called me to assist her. I was gone for about an hour. When I returned, there were several coins lying in the bottom of the hole. I retrieved them and gave them to my mother. These gifts were never large but they were enough to buy bread, milk or other groceries.

I cannot recall what the father in the family on the other side of us did for a living. The son worked at the N&W Railway Company in Roanoke for many years. According to what one of the sons told me, they apparently had a small amount of money. They once owned the house where we lived. I believe my father bought the house for $800.

In any event, we got along well with our neighbors. At that time, everyone worked together and played together all contributing to our quality of life.

More Work

There were many work crews doing various jobs repairing streets, drainage ditches and parks around the mountain areas surrounding Roanoke. In many cases workers dug graves for the deceased. Some folks made fun of the workers and said unkind things about the work crews. However these crews did what they were hired to do, following their supervisors' instructions. The bottom line was to earn money.

These were not the good old days but as optimistic youth, we believed better things were in the making as we looked to the future. While I was a high school student, my own time for work was limited to Saturdays and Sundays

My brothers and I learned that the town of Vinton had openings for street and curb sweepers, among other odd jobs. We applied to the town manager for work. Since he knew us, he was willing to hire us even though we were students. We agreed to his conditions of fifteen cents an hour.

On Saturdays we loaded trucks with trash from various places around town. The trash was in heavy fifty-gallon oil drums, which took two of us to lift up to the bed of the truck and pour out. The truck had two-by-eight-inch boards on the sides to make the bed higher so more trash could be piled in it.

On Sundays we swept the curbs and gutters and carried the trash to the dump. Also on Sundays, I worked at a service station pumping gas, fixing flat tires, changing oil and greasing and washing automobiles. I worked from six to eight hours at the service station and earned $1.50 for the entire day.

It was important for us to fill any available time we had with work, especially during the summer. Fortunately, the town manager let us work in the summer for the same amount of money we earned during the school year. There were ditches to dig, gravel to haul and place into potholes in the roads, then hot tar to spread to smooth the rough automobile rides. We also cleared underbrush on town property to make room for burying water and sewer lines. We worked eagerly to accomplish each of these jobs.

A number of times it was my job to control the nozzle of the hot tar tank which sprayed the tar on the roadway. In the summer the temperature usually hovered around ninety degrees or more and the tar boiled in the kettle in order to run through the hose and out the nozzle. Between the summer heat and the tar kettle with its fire going full blast to make the tar easy to spray, it was extremely hot and messy.

We wore old shoes and trousers until they had to be thrown away. We kept these items separate from other clothes because neither could be used for anything else after this procedure with the hot tar.

At that time, all roads were built or renovated by hand but a grader pulled by a small tractor did the leveling if a truckload of gravel or sand was dumped in one spot. The blade of the grader was rather small but it could accomplish many chores faster than doing the job by hand. Still, because there was so much work to do and workers were limited, we speeded up the process by using rakes and shovels along with the grader.

A tractor with treads later replaced the truck pulling a grader. The older workers driving the grader sometimes came close to pulling up a fire hydrant or a gas or water line buried in the ground but they always took corrective action and stopped in time.

A mistake of that kind when digging a trench or hole during this type of precise construction would have been awful, especially when it came to explaining it to the town manager. Today, to keep accidents to a minimum, we have blueprints available to help workers avoid buried lines.

Before water and sewer pipes could be installed, ditches had to be dug by pick and shovel. Groups of workers went to a location with specifications for accomplishing the job. Usually, before the ditches could be dug, trees and underbrush had to be removed, using axes, scythes and a crosscut saw.

In the early days, the roads were mostly dirt and mud but eventually gravel was spread manually, then hot tar was sprayed on the gravel. In some cases we mixed the gravel and hot tar first, then placed it on the road especially in the holes. In an attempt to smooth the road, we filled a metal drum with water and rolled it over the roadway, either pulling it by hand or by tractor. About five years later, a gasoline engine operated the heavy roller.

It must be remembered that we were working and earning money for our family to survive. Looking back on our childhood, I sometimes wonder in complete amazement how we ever managed to stay alive or, for that matter, how we managed to stay healthy without any medicine or any funds.

As we progressed in our work and demonstrated our responsible and trustworthy natures, our employer recognized our maturity and the town of Vinton gave us additional work.

During the late 1930s, Vinton began to build sidewalks, and each family had to pay for the footage of concrete in front of its house. Since our family did not have the funds to pay for a new sidewalk, we received permission to work off the bill by working for the town.

In those days there were no cement or concrete factories. We had to haul in sand and gravel and mix it with cement and water in a large, homemade wooden box. We mixed it all together with shovels, hoes and rakes. There were no cranes, end loaders or backhoes to lift these heavy items. Muscle power was the order of the day.

After we dug trenches in the dirt, we built sidewalk forms for an entire square block to keep the concrete contained in the exact place we wanted to have a sidewalk. We moved the concrete by wheelbarrow to the wooden forms and dumped it in. A wheelbarrow filled with concrete weighs about three hundred pounds, making it difficult to guide to where we wanted it to go. Of course we tried not to overfill it with concrete because then we could not guide it properly.

Finishing the concrete to make it smooth and suitable for walking was difficult as well. It required two or three men. We'd work at another job for a few hours while the concrete mixture dried enough to begin finishing it properly. The older employees taught us these jobs and others until the next school session began.

There was a tough, mean, foul-talking, heavy-drinking man named Riley who worked for the town at that time. No one spoke mean or ugly words to Riley unless he wanted to fight him then and there. But Riley and I had a good rapport and one Saturday morning he was placed under my supervision while he was serving a number of days' jail time for drunkenness.

I was told to take him with me to the train depot, unload fireplugs from a boxcar and deliver them to a storage lot in the town. According to the bill of laden we were given, the fireplugs weighed five hundred pounds each.

We backed the truck up to the door of the boxcar and prepared to unload the fireplugs. There were two other workers helping us and after getting two fireplugs into the truck, one of them said something about the lightness of the fireplugs and that I was not pulling my weight. As usual the talk got hot and heavy.

I told Riley that I would take one end of the fireplug if he would take the other end and we would load it on the truck. He and the others made remarks about this comment. But he agreed and stepped up to the boxcar door. I walked over to the other side and without a word he and I loaded the fireplug on the truck bed, a distance of about two feet from the railway car.

From then on Riley and I became good friends and he made it known to all who hung around the corner on Main Street that if anyone bothered me he would make sure they would never forget it. I lost track of Riley when the war years came. All I can say is that when he was sober, no man could outwork him as a laborer or beat him in a fistfight.

Other competitions came up from time to time to give us the opportunity to prove ourselves. Once, my two brothers and I were timed by the foreman to see how long it would take us to load number-nine gravel into a truck. Two of us shoveled on each side of the truck and the other shoveled from the back as the timing began. As I recall we loaded the truck to overflowing in twelve minutes. All I can say of this feat was that it really took the steam out of us.

Later, after I'd been instructed to haul material in the truck to various places, I became a regular driver. Then one day a new town manager asked me about my license. When I said I did not have one, he instructed me to take the truck to the Department of Motor Vehicles in Roanoke to get one. At that time, to get a license, each driver had to parallel park a vehicle. I assumed that I must park the truck as if it were an automobile.

I took the inspector around the block to prove that I could drive the truck. I knew he didn't like sitting in the dirty old thing. He told me to let him out at the corner where he would watch me park. I did as I was told. Then I accompanied him inside where he wrote me a license without another word. I don't know if I was the only person who ever parked a dump truck the same as one would have to park a car in order to get a license, but I did it.

Hard work often left me feeling tired and disappointed but there was always the glimmer of light at the end of the tunnel because we never gave up hope. We never became discouraged because our mother gave us inspiration and words of encouragement. Always in our minds we were helping our family to survive, and that made us all the more determined.

When I could not get work with the town of Vinton, I decided to learn how to install a roof and asked Carroll Dooley, my friend's father, to hire me. He had a business replacing metal roofs on houses and businesses and he needed helpers. I was twelve or fourteen years old at the time. I believe the wages were fifteen cents an hour, provided I did not damage any of the metal roofs. Mr. Dooley was the First Sergeant of a reserve army unit in Vinton. He told us about the First World War, when he'd fought in France.

Mr. Dooley's two brothers worked with him but because they would drink over the weekend we could never count on them to be present for work on Monday morning.

Mr. Dooley had a Model-T Ford truck, which was slow but dependable once it was running. The magneto that produced current to the spark plugs had to be set just right prior to using the hand crank to start the truck. If we failed to turn the crank properly, it would kick back with such a force that it could break an arm.

Once when I drove this truck, I forgot to keep my foot off the reverse pedal located between the brake and clutch. This did not cause any damage to the truck but for the others who knew about this pedal, it became a topic for kidding me. We all had a good laugh about it.

In repairing a roof, first hot tar had to be placed on it. Then tarpaper was laid down in a certain manner so that another wiping of the mop filled with hot tar could be applied. Once when we were making repairs to a roof on the local drugstore, I forgot about the second wiping. When I reached down to adjust the edge of the paper in a different position, the hot tar mop wiped my hand. Immediately all the skin came off. It took about a month for my hand to heal.

At times we had to throw tools to each other – a dangerous thing to do because if we dropped a tool, it could put a hole in the roof. Anyone responsible for a hole in the roof would have to repair it at his own expense.

When replacing or repairing a metal roof, we used a wooden mallet because we could not strike tin with a hammer. To shape the tin we used a heavy piece of metal with different heights on either side. First we bent the tin against the higher side, then against the shorter side for the final crimping. This made a solid seam to keep the water from going into the building.

We also used another tool – our weight – to crimp a long section of metal. Both methods provided a seal to keep the water out of the building. Mr. Dooley also had a brake used to bend metal to nail on the roof. We all became proficient in using this brake to make many pieces of metal to fit all kinds of roofs. Eventually however, the roofing business began to falter and with very little work for me to do, our income was reduced.

Rumors of War

During the late 1930s and especially during the early part of 1940, we continually heard the troubling news spreading throughout the world. We heard this verbally from others, as we did not own a radio and could not afford to take the newspaper.

After high school, many young men joined the military services. This became a sad time in the small town of Vinton. However we all knew it would come to this following the attack on Pearl Harbor by the Japanese on December 7, 1941. My time for the military would finally come in September 1942.

Most of us, encouraged by our parents and families, attempted to get our high school diplomas, then go on to find jobs in the business world locally or in the Roanoke area. We hoped to remain close to our friends while bettering our standard of living and assuring that our family members had wholesome food.

Some of our friends applied for college. Continuing education was important to most families, especially if they could afford the cost but at that time this was not an option for me because of our poor financial status. Still, our mother encouraged us to study everything that would get us ahead in the business world.

This is not to discount our father who also attempted to guide us toward learning. However he was not one to favor sports or take interest in any activities that did not produce food and clothing for the family. Our father spent many hours attempting to get better jobs and more funds for the purchase of these needed items, but the lack of work continued to haunt him.

At this time our country was getting over the Depression and people began to have an easier time. But these few months passed rapidly as talk of war and the prospects of everyone getting into the conflict entered our household conversations.

My mother said she was not ready or willing for her sons to go to war and could not understand why people had to fight and kill each other. But she had no control over it. We all prepared as best we knew how for the time to come when we three older boys would be called to join the military and participate in the war. Generally speaking however, we didn't want to go. This was something new and frightful to us.

The continued rumors about the war throughout the world grew more intense daily. However, prospects of limited employment for many adults increased as some of the businesses needed more workers to complete certain jobs.

These businesses would advertise by word of mouth or with placards on telephone poles. The work brought money for households to spend on their many needs and wants. The amount of pay was small but welcome. The work was irregular but it brought hope to people and was a joy to those who had struggled so many years living from hand to mouth. Now there was a light at the end of the tunnel as we all thought about the funds we could earn.

My father was hired as a machine attendant for a furniture company. He was extremely happy for this change in our condition. He said that now he could earn a few dollars, pay off our debts and finish rebuilding our house.

After my graduation from high school, the word around town was that no war would take place and everyone should find reliable employment. I submitted my application for employment with the Roanoke Iron Works, a company that was hiring people to help build boat parts from iron plates. Increased demand for construction led me there and I subsequently learned some of these plates would be used to build ships.

My original application was as an apprentice in the company's drafting department. However there were no vacancies there and I was turned over to the shop superintendent who informed me that my work would be monitored very closely.

Older men, who served as department heads, delighted in bossing the younger persons, yelling at them and commanding them to do certain jobs. They were eager to inform me that I must comply with one important thing before I could get on the payroll. I had to join the union.

At this job, no worker could sit down at any time except during the thirty-minute lunch period or after working hours. This included in the restroom, which consisted of three holes in the floor with water running under them. This arrangement was apparently to ensure that no person could sit even while taking care of the necessities.

At Roanoke Iron Works my responsibility was to move iron plates from one place to another so they could be welded together to form the side of a ship. Huge hooks attached by cables to an electric motor high in the ceiling lifted the plates. Then the motor was pushed along by manpower on an overhead roller to the appropriate place for welding or cutting.

The "bull gang," as we were called, did this type of work. There was no complaint from me because I was working and earning money. At that time, I believed that I was rich and did not have a care in the world.

These huge iron plates were either one-half or three-quarters of an inch thick, weighed more than a ton and if pushed improperly, could decapitate the worker who was trying to move them. They would swing around in the air while the worker tried to get them into place for movement to another section for assembly or shipment. We had to be very careful moving such heavy material.

The foreman in charge was mean, cranky and foul-mouthed. When he gave instructions, he demanded exact responses and if he caught a man sitting down on the job, he would fire him in a heartbeat. He required us to report for work on time and accepted no excuses. If from time to time, some of the older workers did report for work late, they were yelled and hooted at by the other men until everybody in the shop knew they'd been late. If a worker was late two days in a row, the foreman would fire him on the spot.

During my employment at the Roanoke Iron works, the war started. Every eligible male was ordered to report for the draft and be ready to join the military. We three brothers were no exception and we began to prepare to fight for our country in any way we could.

An injury delayed my entry into the war. In 1939, when I was playing football with school classmates, attempting to make the team as a regular player, I experienced severe pain in my right knee. The coach, who was also the principal of the school, examined my knee. He was not happy with the way I could not bend the knee and at my outcry of pain when he exerted pressure upon the outside of my knee joint. He told me that I should see a doctor.

When I informed my parents, they took me to an orthopedic physician. That was when I again encountered Doctor Hoover who had set my broken arm many years earlier. He told my father that I had a tumor growing in my knee, which had to come out whether or not we had the funds to pay for it because it might be cancerous. Doctor Hoover made the necessary arrangements for me to be admitted to the hospital in Roanoke where he operated on my knee. I was in the hospital for seven days. I have no idea who paid for this medical care.

For almost two months, my ability to walk was limited. I followed the doctor's advice as best I could, but infection set in and I had to go back in the hospital for another week for Dr. Hoover to reopen the incision and drain fluid from the joint. Then he released me with orders to only walk, not run, for at least two more months. He forbade me to play any sports because it would agitate my knee and might be the cause for another operation.

In 1942, with this operation behind me, I passed my physicals for the military draft and was declared fit for service. This suited me just fine because I did not want to remain at home when others were going to war.

PART 2 THE WAR YEARS

The Second Wiseman

Pearl Harbor

During the late 1930s, everyone heard many rumors about the war Japan initiated with China. We all knew something of grave importance was happening but it was hard to determine the exact details because news was slow and not very accurate. Almost every day there were reports of brutal actions by Japanese troops upon the Chinese people, who were murdered for no apparent reason. These were impossible to understand and horrible to hear.

At our young age we were limited in our understanding of what was going on in the world, especially the horrors of killing on a large scale. But the President and representatives informed us in radio announcements that our young boys would not be subjected to such an ordeal and our country would not become involved in the conflict because it was not something concerning us. These world conditions eventually led to our great country's entrance into war, even though our President and Congress denied there would be a war.

We finally entered the 1940s when government programs provided work for people. It was at this time the Civilian Conservation Corps (CCC) became important although it had been started a few years before.

The CCC, along with the Works Progress Administration (WPA), provided work on many projects financed by tax money from the federal government to help the cities and towns toward building a better life for the population. Workers built roads and bridges and cleaned ditches and rivers. Other specific projects included beautifying and enhancing the areas along the Appalachian Trail leading into the mountains toward the Peaks of Otter. Each worker earned income for himself and his family in addition to providing structures everyone could appreciate for years to come.

Some people spoke unfavorably about the WPA, the CCC and other groups working around the county and in the cities, calling them welfare types but the workers were in need of the money to support their families. The agonizing hardships suffered by us and the other families in slow, day-to-day living on mostly nothing had no real end in sight.

At that time I could not figure out where the money was coming from to finance these projects. We young people had very little knowledge of economics, banks or loans. But now I realize that the treasury borrowed from the banks, which were backed by the Federal Reserve Bank after it was formed in the 1930s. There was no intent on the part of any agency to lend funds to private individuals, especially those who had no house or other collateral or any way to make repayment. The entire CCC and WPA provided social welfare; most people called it socialism.

Today the Appalachian Trail stands as a memorial to the WPA and CCC groups who began it and worked so hard to build it. Men cleared trails from Maine to Georgia and placed rest stops where they would do the most good. They built rustic lodges, leaving plenty of room for expansion, out of boards and stanchions cut in the rough and never sanded to a smooth finish, though at times they were stained.

This was a small part of the effort that got the country up from the Great Depression and gave the citizens spirit and energy to go forward. East of Roanoke and Vinton, as one passes on either Route 460 or crosses over the bridge on I-64 and I-81, travelers can see the Appalachian Trail.

As Boy Scouts, we spent weekends in the mountains, clearing brush from these trails in the forest to keep them open. We were not hired to clear the trail. We just did it as a good deed and for the credit of our scout troop. Our activities helped the hikers and others who enjoyed the outdoors.

During the Depression, the CCC and the WPA also built the Peaks of Otter, a resort area near Bedford, Virginia. The Federal Government operates this place for tourists most of the year by providing sleeping arrangements as well as food service.

Once my wife and I were on the top of the mountain at the Peaks of Otter when an ice storm came through, blocking all the roads. The weather was so severe that only cars equipped with chains could get to the top of the mountain if the Park Rangers even permitted people to drive there.

Food was running out and the cabins were cold. There was no place to get warm. As a result everyone was asked to leave following a snowplow that escorted us down slippery roads off the mountain. It was fun while it lasted but we felt relieved when we finally arrived back in Bedford and were glad to be on the road home to Norfolk.

Most voters were in favor of the WPA and CCC because their work made the communities look good and brought money into the households where it was needed. This does not mean that all things constructed by the WPA or CCC were better than other construction but what was accomplished still stands for quality in the minds of most folks. Most workers and the superintendents who directed them on the jobs took pride in their workmanship and pleasure in demonstrating the end product.

However, while our neighbors and friends were as happy as we at getting out from under the dark cover of unemployment and poverty, which had been most degrading to everyone for the past ten to twelve years, the looming war was a heavy load hanging over our heads, and we all felt scared. The world was in a sad turmoil, with fighting ongoing in almost every country. We were concerned about our youth, who were slated to fight in a war they knew nothing about.

At that time the raging war between Japan and China continued with no end in sight. Even today, there is no good reason to explain why Japan invaded China. We can only conclude that the bottom line was greed for land and materials and a desire to expand Japan's borders by defeating China. Greed and domination – these were apparently the reasons Japan also attacked the United States on December 7, 1941.

Those of us who were old enough to understand world affairs were not motivated to get involved in the war in any way unless our country was attacked. We all hoped the evil would pass us by and permit us to live life to the fullest. Most of the conversations with our family members were about our own lives and ways we could earn funds to meet expenses.

Every adult American living on December 7, 1941, remembers when the Japanese struck Pearl Harbor with its mighty forces, bombing everything in sight. The intent was to kill every American in the air or on the ground and to blow up the country, beginning with Hawaii.

This blow changed the nature and complexion of the entire world. At the time, the Japanese and other Asian countries saw the United States as a paper tiger because our military had nearly no manpower. We were considered on a par with third-world countries.

The brave warriors who joined the military after December 7 swelling its ranks to almost overflowing changed this attitude. In addition, this great country entered the European theatre to protect not only Great Britain and other European countries but also to keep the shipping lanes open on the seas of the world.

All these things came together because we, the people, loved this great country and refused to give in to the whim of any dictator. Patriotism was the single thought in the minds of most citizens and military personnel. It fueled a desire to show other countries that we could out-produce and out-maneuver any other power on earth. Winning the war proved this to be true.

I will never forget the day that the Japanese attacked us. I was working at the service station with many customers coming and going when I heard the news. Because of my youth and lack of knowledge of world events, I did not realize the seriousness of the situation. Some people said the U.S. would whip the Japanese in a few weeks and everybody would be happy.

Within a few days we heard that a Japanese plane had twice bombed an area on the west coast near Oregon. This rumor was true but nothing of consequence happened.

Most of us young men, as we talked among each other about our future, were optimistic about the war even though we knew nothing about fighting or killing and had no idea what to expect. Eventually, along with many thousands of other young men, I received my greetings from the draft board in September 1942. My employment at the iron works was held for me and should have been available to me upon my return from the military. Time and circumstances however, changed everything.

I was administered the oath and inducted into the Army at Roanoke that September. I was ordered to report to the train station in Roanoke within thirty days. I immediately began preparing my personal belongings and arranging my papers, making ready for the date of my departure. Since I was living at home and had very little to pack or care for, this was a small task for me.

When I arrived at the station on the scheduled date to report for military duty, there were hundreds of men standing around waiting for the same train, not knowing what to do. But a person in charge of each train car assigned us to a seat as our names were called.

After we boarded the train, all persons were counted. Then the train departed the station and I began my first and most exciting long train ride of my life to our destination at Macon, Georgia.

Most of us were anxious about our futures and talked with each other of our fears, our home life and most especially, what we had been doing for work and play. We were also very interested in seeing the countryside as we passed along the rail track. Most of us had not seen the country outside our area in Virginia and were impressed with the beautiful homes and scenery, which we compared to our own area. We also marveled at the farmland and growing crops.

After fifteen hours we arrived in Atlanta where we changed to another train that took us to Macon. From there we all were bused to different sections at nearby Camp Wheeler. I was assigned to the Sixth Battalion, Company D to undergo thirteen weeks of intensive training.

Basic Training

Our introduction to the military was loud, harsh and demanding at every second. At our assigned barracks, a sergeant gave the orders for all to obey. We marched double time, running as fast as we could to the dispensary where medical teams gave us shots and took vital information. Then a doctor gave us an examination to determine that we were alive.

Afterward, we ran to a supply warehouse where clothing was issued. We packed up all of our civilian clothing and mailed it back home because no civilian clothing was allowed.

The next morning at four a.m., we awoke to a bugle call and assembled outside for roll call. On our second day we answered questions and filled out forms all day long. Then on the third day, we awakened as usual but on this day we began our training, running and exercising as fast as we could with no excuses accepted.

We began training in small groups, marching and learning to take orders. Each day we were trained in infantry, rifle range, heavy and special weapons and bayonets. We were told when to eat when to sleep and when to train.

Prior to going on the rifle range, we had dry firing practice. Instructors walked behind us, telling how to hold the rifle in every position in order to hit the target. This type of training lasted about three days. Then the following morning at 6:00 a.m., we reported to the rifle range.

At the rifle range we loaded the rifle with live rounds of ammunition and fired at a target about a hundred yards away. The non-commissioned officers (NCOs) carefully instructed us on how to fire the weapon. Then the target was inspected after each section had fired.

Next, our target was moved to two hundred yards, then three hundred yards. If we did not get good scores, we remained at the range or returned later for more practice.

From the target range we marched to the obstacle course. Here we had to run, dodging certain embankments and climbing make-believe fences using ropes attached to the top to pull ourselves upward. Metal and concrete pipes lying on the ground forced us to crawl, all the while carrying our weapon, which we had to keep clean and dry. With live ammunition being fired over us, we crawled through barbed wire to get to the end of the course. Once a soldier crawled through a snake's den on his way to the end of the course. In his fright, he stood up. Live machine gun rounds went through him before the command could be given to cease firing. We recruits witnessing his death learned that obeying orders was most important. The life we saved might be our own.

Our job was to preserve our lives and attempt to kill the enemy. This training brought home to me and my friends just how fragile life can be. Above all it taught us to be more resilient in defending ourselves.

We learned how to fire mortar rounds, 30- and 50-caliber machine guns, rifles and 45-caliber automatic hand pistols. We learned how to kill the enemy silently, with almost any kind of weapon including a K-bar knife, which we also used to open our boxed meals.

Our intense training made time seem to stop so that all we knew was whether it was day or night. Our days, each one different, began at 4:30 in the morning.

I shall never forget the bayonet practice we received – severe to those of us who were new to the acts of warfare. We pretended that a man was in front of us attempting to kill us with his bayonet and we had to thrust, strike, push and pull our bayonet into a dummy with just the correct penetration to kill him.

We received diagrams of what would happen to the man when we thrust the bayonet correctly. We learned that the cupped sides of the bayonet would create a vacuum and as the bayonet was withdrawn, the intestines automatically would come out with the bayonet. We practiced this bayonet method at every turn of our training. We became quite proficient, earning high instructor's ratings.

We thought that if a person fell, he would not hurt us after that because he would be incapacitated; however we later learned this was not entirely true. We learned to make sure that the enemy soldier was dead, never to turn our backs on him, even though he was on the ground because he could still kill us prior to his dying. In essence we were trained killers.

During this time, I remember the constant drilling of the troops. The instructors were precise and very demanding. Superiors graded them about once each week when there was a regimental parade.

Each company received a position, and we learned how to march holding our bodies straight, never bobbing our heads, looking straight ahead unless instructed otherwise by the platoon leaders. One sergeant, to ensure that he was marching properly, asked me to look at the back of his head and tell him if he moved it right or left.

Once we learned this disciplined method we began to work and march together as a team. Teamwork counts when confronted by enemy soldiers. In fact, this is what saves lives.

Even though we all were U.S. soldiers, two groups formed and we took turns being the enemy for training purposes. Each side became the aggressor as the training advanced. One of our duties was to learn how to avoid being detected while we penetrated enemy lines at night through mud and rain. We tried to keep the other group from locating us or making us look bad. Either way, both sides learned how to act in these circumstances.

At first, after the end of each day's training, most of us were too tired to go out into Macon. However, we soon became used to the training and eventually ventured into the city. Of course, we met many girls. We had fun learning how to dance, and above all, learning how to treat young ladies at the USO.

I remember the song "I Left My Heart at the Stage Door Canteen," which was very popular at the time:

> Old Mister Absent-Minded, that's me –
> Just as forgetful as I can be.
> I've got the strangest sort of a mind;
> I'm always leaving something behind.

> I left my heart at the Stage Door Canteen.

I left it there with a girl named Eileen.

I kept her serving doughnuts
'Till all she had were gone.
I sat there dunking doughnuts
'Till she caught on.

I must go back to the army routine
And every doughboy knows what that will mean.

A soldier boy without a heart
Has two strikes on him from the start.
And my heart's at the Stage Door Canteen.*

Following our night out, we were ordered back to the rigorous training the next morning regardless of the number of beers we'd had or other excuses we could give to keep us from actively training.

Most training activities were sprung on us at a moment's notice with each session supervised. I remember learning to handle live dynamite, which except for having to light a fuse, substituted for hand grenades. We learned how to throw these simulated grenades where they would be most effective. Later, we received live grenades and learned how to throw them without hurting ourselves or anyone around us.

One of our instructors, a tough sergeant who'd been a member of the U.S. Army for about eight years, always tried to intimidate everyone he trained. He was placed in a very uncomfortable position when some of the recruits became angry with him and with the Army.

Each Friday, all bunks had to be moved while the entire barracks floor was scrubbed and all footlockers and clothing were

---

* Words and Music by Irving Berlin. This Is The Army, Inc., NYC, 1942.
From the Popular American Sheet Music Collection, Department of Special Collections, Miller Nichols Library, UMKC, Kansas City.

inspected. One of those times the recruits felt angry over the quality and quantity of our food rations. They also wanted to get out of cleaning the barracks.

They said they could not wait for the war to end so they could get back home. But they were not satisfied with just talking. They made their anger known by attempting to destroy the barracks, breaking furniture, beds and other Army property.

This tough sergeant kept up a continuing dialogue with me and some of the other soldiers. Maybe he was looking for someone he could trust. I do know that he demanded the troops be punished because they damaged some of the barracks and failed to pass inspection. Because the culprit who began the outburst could not be identified, he chose me to discipline the entire company.

I marched the entire company around the quadrangle that encompassed three other companies. This included two hours of close-order drill in the center of the quadrangle as well as marching around the entire battalion area. There was a lot of grumbling but the message came through loud and clear.

From then on I could get the sergeant as well as the company officer (CO) to agree to almost anything. In fact the sergeant and I became friends after this and we visited the city together. He changed my name to Bill for some odd reason and continued to call me that until we all were transferred to different places.

Even though most of the troops were older than I, this sergeant chose me to teach the other men how to evade the enemy at night. Following his instructions, I taught them how to move fast in the dark without alerting the enemy of our presence. He instructed us to choose a path upon which the enemy had not traveled. These were simulated hunt-and-destroy actions that we practiced when we were on maneuvers.

We wore camouflage clothing and were ordered to penetrate the other group's headquarters by any means possible, short of firing our weapons or causing any U.S. soldier bodily harm. The object of this training was to teach infantry men to stay alive while killing the enemy in the process. But the primary objective was to capture the enemy for interrogation.

Of course we did not try to kill our own soldiers. However, there were times when short-tempered people fussed and fumed and cussed about the silliest things, complaining about the weather or how dull the training base was.

Regularly, we were called out for twenty-mile forced marches with full field equipment. For our own protection, someone always checked each of us for the proper equipment.

These trips included obstacle courses with live ammunition fired over our heads. Generally we had to crawl through dynamite fields without knowing when an explosion would occur. A nearby instructor hidden from sight detonated the dynamite. This training simulated mortars or artillery fire.

On these marches we were never sure when we would return or where we would be at night. If we saw the cook driving toward us we knew that an all-night training was in order. We were furnished with compasses and given destinations to cover and reports to make when we returned. Each group was small and as always there was someone in charge to keep us from cheating or to ensure that we knew what to do if we should become lost.

Once my group came within six feet of another group's command post and later, we reported who was present and what they had discussed at that time. This report surprised the other group leaders, who never knew we were anywhere around their area.

We stayed outside and slept on the ground, though sometimes we were fortunate to sleep in a pup tent if it was raining. Generally when we got wet or cold we had to walk or run in order to get our clothing dry. During the entire period of WW II, the only way to sleep was on the ground, regardless of the weather. After we left the training barracks and went overseas, there were no more warm places to sleep.

The most important items to an infantryman or ground trooper were his shoes and his weapon – with ammunition, of course. How well shoes fit was especially important because with no vehicle, we had to depend on our feet for transportation.

Once while in training, I received a new pair of shoes. The sergeant instructed me to stand in a foot-deep puddle of water for about a half hour. Then I marched around the battalion until my shoes dried out. This not only caused my shoes to dry but to fit my feet properly with no pain at all.

After about thirteen weeks, our basic training was complete and the groups were divided into transfer units to be shipped out to join a division or go to another camp. We never knew in advance where we would go or which outfit we would join. The emphasis was placed on the troops getting trained quickly.

I was fortunate in a manner of speaking, to remain at Camp Wheeler teaching new recruits how to become fighting soldiers. During this period, my responsibilities increased to handling not only personnel but ensuring that the soldiers received their mail along with any information from the First Sergeant and Company Commander. Some of my responsibilities also involved teaching the soldiers how to march, shoot and avoid capture. On the forced marches competition was keen to meet each platoon's objectives. At times there would be a ringer thrown in just to see what we would do under changed circumstances.

We were in Company D, the battalion weapons unit. We received extensive weapons training on the Browning automatic rifle, both 60- and 80-mm mortars and the .03 Springfield rifle.

Shortly thereafter we were issued the M-1, which held eight rounds as opposed to the .03, which held five rounds. The M-1 had more firepower but was not an automatic rifle, as most thought. Also, it loaded faster and the entire clip automatically ejected when the last round was fired. This meant that extra bulky ammunition had to be carried but in the long run having the extra firepower was worth the effort.

It was around November 1943 when we learned that all personnel who had completed their training (including me) would be transferred overseas. However, I was held back on orders of the CO.

The first sergeant called me to his office and said that the CO wanted to speak to me. When I arrived in his office, the CO said that the regimental commander wanted me to attend officer-candidate school (OCS) at Fort Benning, Georgia.

He spent more than an hour attempting to convince me to attend the school, speaking highly of my motivation, explaining what I would accomplish and stating the Army needed people like me. But I disappointed him by declining the offer, as I did not want to make the Army a career. I was classed as a citizen soldier and believed that this was the correct decision for me.

The war was heating up, with more and more troops needed overseas. We continued to train and instruct new soldiers for the great push that was coming. Every day we were bombarded with information to prepare the soldiers for this. It had already started with the invasion of North Africa and the projection was that next it would be France or somewhere in Europe.

If anyone knew the site of the invasion, it was never discussed. Everyone knew that "loose lips sink ships." As 1943 was coming to an end and all of us were thinking about Christmas leave with our families, we were ordered to refrain from discussing any activities regarding troop movements.

I requested and received fifteen days leave to go home to visit my parents. A few months prior to this time, I met Marie Deery, a girl in Macon. Her father served on active duty out of the Boston area as a commander in the Navy. We had a nice, comfortable relationship but when I informed her of my fifteen days leave, she was upset. However knowing the military, she accepted the situation and said she would be waiting for me to return.

I traveled by Greyhound bus from Macon to Atlanta, Georgia then to Roanoke, a fifteen-hour trip that afforded me time for thought regarding Marie and our relationship. She wanted to get married.

From Roanoke I rode a streetcar to Vinton. While I was home I informed my parents that I had been seeing Marie and discussed her as well as her family. I assured them that I would not do anything rash but wait until after the war before Marie and I made a decision on marriage. My parents found this acceptable.

During my leave I visited my grandparents and a few relatives but mostly I remained at home with my parents. The days moved quickly and then it was time for me to return to Camp Wheeler.

During those many hours on the bus, both going and coming, I had lots of time to think about my future and I decided that I would not marry Marie. This decision was based mostly on her family background, which was financially better than mine

When I finally arrived back in Macon, Marie was still upset because she had not gone with me to meet my family. I explained that she would have had to stay in a hotel or similar place because there was no room at my parents' house. I declined to tell her that the house was not completed because of the fire.

Marie and I talked about the war and what would happen to us if and when I returned to the United States. Later, when I told her I was being transferred from Camp Wheeler, she became quite upset but finally realized that the military sent troops where it wanted them to go. She was already planning to visit Vinton to meet my parents during the summer of 1944 provided she could get the time off from her employment at the local bank.

Many months later when I was in France, I received letters from my mother and from an aunt telling me that Marie had visited the area. They were impressed with her and spoke highly of her education and high morals. However my aunt wrote that her thoughts were aligned with mine concerning what I had been thinking about a marriage between Marie and me. "Do not hurry into a marriage," she advised, "and think carefully of your future."

Additionally, this same aunt said that Marie and her family lived within an inch of their money, which was contrary to my upbringing. Instilled in my mind from the earliest years was how we only had the financial resources to provide food for the entire family.

Overseas Transfer

In March 1944, I received orders to report to Fort Mead, Maryland preparatory to being transferred to the European theatre overseas. After two days at Fort Meade with many others under the same orders, we went by bus to New York where we boarded a Liberty ship tied up at one of the piers. I do not recall the name of the ship, but I know it was filled to capacity with soldiers, ammunition and weapons.

It was around midnight when we boarded the ship. We learned through the ship's crewmembers that this ship would join a convoy already underway coming from the south.

All we Army personnel wanted to know was where we would land and what would be there at the landing site; but the sailors, with whom we had limited contact, did not know this information. There was much talk about how stable and seaworthy the ship was. Finally we departed New York and embarked onto the vast Atlantic Ocean, which I had never seen before. We were prohibited from smoking or having lights in the open.

For the next seventeen miserable days and nights, seasickness made me hope that I would either die or get to dry land. During the voyage I worked in the galley cleaning pots and pans, which only added to my seasickness. The severe rolling movements of the ship made my life extremely uncomfortable, to say the least.

When we ate a meal in the galley, we had to stand at a table rather than sit down because there were so many military men to feed in the mess area. The trays of food would slide away from us unless we held on with one hand while trying to eat with the other.

The smell of food made me ill and I spent most of my time throwing up anything in my stomach. After about three or four days, we sailed into a storm in the North Atlantic and this extra movement of the ship caused me to remain violently sick.

We learned that the ship was entering a hurricane area. We were ordered to wear life jackets twenty-four hours a day and be prepared to abandon ship if the orders were given. I tried everything including drinking salt water to get rid of my seasickness but nothing worked and I continued to vomit.

Once during the voyage, all personnel were placed on alert when we heard of a submarine in the area. Flags and lights transferred messages from ship to ship when visibility and the nearness of the vessels permitted. I saw these blinking lights from the other ships, as well as the one I was on, during my many trips outside in the air attempting to get rid of the seasickness. The submarine sighting was startling, not only to the ship's crew but also to those of us who believed we had as safe a trip as was possible with the other ships surrounding us as we traveled.

Our convoy of about fifteen ships traveled slowly through the wild and rough seas toward our destination at a speed of about twelve knots. The waves were so high they almost submerged us, especially when huge waves struck from all sides at the same time. The waves rolled us back and forth until we had no idea which direction the ship was headed.

My seasickness caused me to lose my ability to walk, talk straight or read. I was completely lost. When I asked the medical personnel about my condition they just laughed and said I would get over it. It was not life threatening. But to me, it felt worse than death.

On the last day at sea, we prepared to disembark but we were not informed where we would land. The other vessels departed from us during the night. Then we saw a dimly-lit shoreline. We were not allowed on deck unless ordered, nor were we given any information regarding our destination. Not until the ship docked did we learn we were in Glasgow, Scotland and the time was around midnight. Then we were instructed to get our gear and when ordered, to leave the ship quickly.

We hustled to a train, its engine already running as it awaited our arrival. Then began the long ride toward the south of England according to the rumors we received from the train crew. In fact, as no person in authority told us, we did not know exactly where the train was headed.

The train's route south was circuitous, slow and extremely cold. The night was dark and foggy. Rain was falling. We discussed how there was no comparison between this type of transportation here and in the United States. Even though England was many years older, ours was superior.

After ten to twenty hours on the train, we were too exhausted to realize how tired, hungry and thirsty we were. Finally though, the train stopped and we were ordered off at a very small station. Though being without food or water was new for us then, we quickly learned that hunger and thirst would be our constant companions for the next several months.

From the train station, we hurriedly marched to a training compound composed of a group of tents and a few wooden buildings with lights that could not be detected from the outside. When daylight came we were able to see that what we thought were a few tents were really many. Each tent held about eight people.

When we entered the first flap we found a second flap was there to keep any light from filtering through to the outside that might be seen by enemy aircraft personnel overhead. We were ordered not to light any fires and above all not to smoke.

Within the tent city, we discovered we had joined units of the 29th Infantry Division, which was crowded in with other military units. We trained daily with one of these units as well as with the First Infantry Division. We did not have time to think or do anything except take orders. It appeared everyone was in a hurry and we knew that the invasion was uppermost in the minds of all military personnel.

Training began at 4 a.m. the morning we arrived, leaving us very little time for sleep. We were not allowed to go anywhere except to the chow line and toilet while we continued to train. The first item in our training was to become accustomed to the weather. It continued to rain.

We lived in this muddy tent city with very few boards to walk on. It was a constant challenge in the ever-present mud to keep our feet dry. We stayed wet almost the entire time we were in England.

Our training continued what had been started in the U.S. – firing the rifle and machine gun, throwing hand grenades, marching and drilling.

As we learned near the end of the war, our mission was to be cannon fodder for German machine guns at Normandy when the invasion began. However, the plans were changed when the 29th Division was finally selected to start the invasion. Their regiment, the 116th Infantry, led the way to the beach.

At that time none of us knew where the landing would be but we knew it was imminent. None of us was permitted to leave the training area. There was no leave of any kind, only training and more training.

Physicians and psychiatrists interviewed us, and maybe a psychologist as well. The interviews were conducted around the clock because of the large number of personnel. One of my many interviews occurred well after dark because I had difficulty locating the correct medical tent.

The long hikes with full field packs and practice on the rifle ranges continued in the ever-present rain, consuming every minute of our time. Repeatedly medical personnel and all our superiors instructed that if we were captured we should only give our name, rank and serial number and say no more.

We received special clothing that would offer some protection if the Germans used mustard gas or any chemical in an attempt to capture or kill us. Our gas masks were regular-issue equipment as a part of our backpacks.

The people in charge overlooked no detail in divesting us of any identifying papers in our possession. We placed all our letters and identification papers in envelopes addressed to our homes in the U.S. If we had address books, we either had to dispose of them or send them back to our homes as well. The only identification we were allowed to carry with us was our dog tags.

The local people around our training area never saw us. They only knew that day and night troops marched on some roads and jeeps, tanks and trucks drove by.

Each night, we heard the sirens sounding for many hours warning us of aircraft flying over and bombing the areas. We knew that the English protected our position from airplanes flying over the area with cables held aloft by balloons. I heard this worked very well for downing aircraft when they flew into the cables.

The time passed quickly from our arrival in April and before we knew what was happening, we were collecting all of our gear, including our rifles, ammunition and gas masks and boarding a truck bound for Southampton, England about one hour from the training area. When we arrived at the docks, we boarded a ship. This was June 1944.

We knew what was coming, and we expected the worst. We placed our issued K-rations and candy bars in our pockets and packs. The candy bars were so hard it took almost a day just to eat one but they were delicious.

Normandy Invasion

It took days of preparation to get the ships loaded and ready to move out with all the troops gathered aboard. But finally we gathered near the ships on the piers around 9 to 10 o'clock in the evening. We were told not to smoke, show any lights or flash any gear that could be seen by the enemy aircraft personnel. These aircraft were flying over our positions every night taking pictures and attempting to locate movement of our troops.

We finally boarded the ships around 2 or 3 o'clock in the morning. The ships were crammed with troops with no space to move. We had to squeeze by another person to go to the bathroom, which we could only do with permission.

Within two hours the ship got underway. We had no knowledge what part of Europe we would be seeing when we landed but we learned that the 29th Division had already landed at Normandy a few days earlier. They were in serious trouble with enemy machine gun and artillery fire.

Our aircraft constantly flying overhead bombed the coast of France prior to the ships moving out into the Channel. This bombing neutralized the gun emplacements and paved the way for the soldiers' landing. German aircraft flew over us only at night but they were few because the great number of U.S. aircraft may have worried the general staff of the German Army.

When our ship moved out from the piers, we could not see anything but fog and drizzle. The ship's crew began to discuss the 29th Division landing. They told us the news coming by radio from ships at the landing area. The invasion had begun with the landing in Normandy, France at 0400 hours. It was June 7, 1944.

The crossing to France took about four or five hours because the convoy was so huge that each ship had to wait for those ahead to discharge troops. Meanwhile, air strikes were ongoing with hundreds of aircraft flying overhead.

Ships with soldiers and Navy personnel aboard stretched out as far as the eye could see, projecting awesome might to the enemy's eye. In fact, anyone who saw it would never forget how awesome it was with the sun lighting up the sky toward the east, with bursts of light from cannon and artillery fire and from the aircraft bombings. We were not in a position to observe the entire operation, but the guns we heard firing from the decks of the ships gave us just a glimmer of the entire strike force.

As our ship finally approached its discharge point, we climbed down rope ladders into landing craft operated by Navy personnel. These boats moved in and out from the beaches as fast as they could. Later I learned the boats were mostly wood from the southern U.S. They were expendable.

The boat I was on stopped about seventy-five yards short of the beach. The front end of the boat had a ramp higher than the body of the boat, which a sailor lowered into the water. Then we moved out toward the beach. The ramp was not visible in the water. We went in well above our waists forcing us to keep our rifles and ammunition held high. By this time it was early afternoon and we knew darkness would overtake us unless we got off very fast.

We had to get to the beach before we were killed or injured from incoming shells. The constant loud noise prevented us from understanding what was happening. We had to remember what we were taught during our training and do it.

Bodies of soldiers and sailors floated in the water around us, along with pieces of landing boats and airplane parts. In fact, based upon the bodies we saw and the material floating by us, it appeared to us that no American soldier had yet reached the beach.

The shore batteries fired on every ship as well as on the smaller boats going to shore. The big guns on the ships in the convoy fired back at the enemy hidden behind barricades on shore attempting to knock out the machine guns, artillery pieces and fortifications built by the Germans.

Although the firing was less intense at this time because the first waves of troops had landed, I shall always remember the deafening noise of the artillery and ships' guns. When we looked up toward the sky, we could see the huge missiles from the ships' guns going toward the shore. When they exploded, we could see the earth and parts of the concrete barricades built around the gun emplacements fly upward. Many people shouted orders, mostly yelling for us to get to the shore fast.

Sure we were scared. We prayed a lot – mostly to ourselves – and kept going toward shore. We believed that God was with us. At that moment there were no atheists; all of us prayed over and over. Some prayed out loud. None of us were shy, and we each admitted a fear of dying because we did not know what was on the other side of life.

The noise from the guns was so loud no person could hear himself even if he yelled at the top of his voice. I, along with many other veterans, now suffer hearing loss as a result of the noise from the guns that never stopped firing until the end of the war. We had no earplugs. We were told this was one of the facts of life in a war.

After we gained the beach, we marched single file along a narrow pathway up the beach. Aside from the guns firing from the ships and the shore batteries, the first evidence of military activity on shore were signs in German warning of land mines.

ACHTUNG MEINEN

We entered the wooded brush on a path toward a regrouping area that had been designated prior to the landing. The path led to Sault St. Marie, a small village of five or six houses within a few hundred yards of the beach. We marched around the churchyard of a small church, Ste. Mère-Église.

As we moved forward, we saw fortifications in flooded fields with high, pointed sticks of wood or iron protruding into the air. These fortifications prevented paratroopers from surviving their jumps. It also stopped gliders from landing safely. We saw many wrecked gliders lying in the water or on the ground as a result of striking these fortifications. The background made it difficult for the landing troops to see these fortifications from the air and the protruding spikes caused terrific damage to our troops. This is what war is all about – killing the enemy wherever he is found.

Jack Howell, one of my friends from Vinton and a paratrooper assigned to the 101st Airborne Division, landed several miles inland of Normandy. He lost a leg when he landed and had to be evacuated from the area. His father was the Chief of Police in Vinton at that time. I did not see him then or know of this incident until after the war when he explained to me where they landed.

When the intent of one group is to shoot and kill another just for the goal of gaining a foothold in another country, then we can say war is hell. There are no words to describe what it's like to walk over or around dead enemies or our own dead soldiers just to get to shelter.

The entire group on the beach moved along at a slow pace trying to locate our assigned divisional units. By this time, only a dozen of us remained because the others had departed to nearby units. A master sergeant named Berlin stopped us, stating he needed some administrative help and asked if any man among us could operate a typewriter. I spoke up but added that it had been quite some time since my high school training.

He led me to a tent under some trees near an embankment where he introduced me to three other men in the tent. Then he gave me some hand-written papers to type, which I had to do by candlelight. I protested that it had been a long time since I had typed but he could find no other person who knew anything about a typewriter. He commanded a replacement battalion of only a very few men awaiting orders to move forward.

We remained in this location for about a week. One day, a Catholic priest stopped by and invited the entire group of eight men to attend church the following Sunday.

Our group, including three new persons who had just arrived, gathered at the church for the Sunday service. It felt strange to most of us to carry our weapons inside the church. The priest instructed us to stack them against the wall adjacent to where we sat.

The priest spoke to the congregation in French and then spoke to us in English. He thanked us for our presence in France and thanked all Americans for helping to get the Germans out of the village. In appreciation, the families present invited us to be their guests for the mid-day meal.

Three of us went with one family who did not speak English and at that time, we did not speak French. However, we got along marvelously well and had an excellent time.

I felt concerned that by serving us a meal, the family may have deprived themselves of food. The meal consisted of very little meat and some potatoes that the farmer's wife had prepared for our benefit and pleasure.

Looking back, I am so proud that we attended the church services and had an opportunity to visit with the French family. We did not stay more than two hours because we knew that our commanding officer would be upset with us. We had one extra glass of wine with the family and then collected our weapons and departed after thanking them again for such good food.

Unfortunately, I did not get their names and by now they have long been deceased. However my memories are extremely pleasant of that meal. In spite of the war going on and the artillery and rifle firing heard in the distance reminding us that Germans were not very far from this house, thoughts of their warm hospitality remain with me to this day reminding me that humanity can thrive in the midst of inhumanity.

St. Lo

Early the next morning, we had other things to consider as we moved out for St. Lo on the road to Paris. Prior to moving out we received military service records of a number of soldiers newly assigned to our unit. To my surprise three of them were from Vinton. I had not seen anyone from there in almost three years.

I took the initiative and kept their records separate, waiting for them to catch up with us because I knew they had to report when they arrived. It must have been just before we reached St. Lo when they caught up with us. They were surprised to find me holding their records. We spent a few good hours chatting about our families and friends still in Vinton and about the times we shared there. We also discussed where they would go and what division they would report to when they departed.

As usual, all good things must come to an end and the following day they were transferred to other units. I personally wished them good luck and was proud to claim them as my friends. One of the men died several years after the war. I have not seen the others for years. I do know that one of them, Shirley Crowder, returned to Vinton and years later became the mayor. Eugene Holmes and Jimmy Fuqua lived just a few blocks from my house and may still be living in Vinton.

We moved east on the way to St. Lo. Some of the troops moved north toward Cherbourg, where General Patton eventually landed his tanks and other armored vehicles. The movement was slow and deliberate with many casualties at every field or open space. Yet the only possible way to advance through the hedgerows was with foot soldiers.

The hedgerows developed naturally when trees and underbrush grew along the sides of the fields. Usually a ditch separated the field from the hedgerows, draining off excess water.

Not every field was plowed. Some were just weeds and brush. But others had been plowed; and although it was June and way past time for sowing seeds, the farmers had not planted crops. These fields were filled with messy, sticky mud that kept us from walking very well. It was no place for a farmer and his mules – or people for that matter.

I do not recall seeing any tractors in the fields but they could not move in the mud any more than the heavy guns could. Only foot soldiers shooting at the Germans with rifles could drive them out of France at such a slow and deliberate pace.

Nightly patrols gathered intelligence about the number of enemy soldiers contacted or observed. This information was passed it on to the commanders who in turn would make decisions as to when and where to attack. Every soldier went on the patrols.

Much later, tanks came in from Cherbourg but they had a rough time navigating because of the soft turf. When they were driven into the hedgerows or ditches, the front ends would rise, exposing them to artillery fire, hand grenades, rocket grenades and especially mortars that knocked them out of action. This kept the tanks from helping defend and protect us. We lost many soldiers caught by the continuous enemy fire when they tried to seek cover near the damaged tanks.

But then, an engineer in the tank unit had a marvelous idea. Using a blade from a caterpillar tractor, he attached it on the front of the tank to deflect the incoming shells. Even better, this invention also served to cut through the underbrush. The tank's powerful engine pushed the blade forward, knocking down trees and brush. Then, using the tank as a protective shield, the infantry could move toward the enemy through this opening in the hedgerow while also relying on the tank's firepower.

The hedgerows were places for troops on both sides to hide and take cover from the artillery, machine gun and rifle fire. We all expected to be caught in the open because the Germans had been practicing for this expected invasion for years and were prepared to fight in any manner to prevent being captured or killed.

Of course, the Germans were tough and well disciplined. They could utilize their 88-mm cannons quite well, waiting for our troops to get into a clearing or on a road. Then they'd zero in, firing on us from their tiger tanks.

This is not to ignore the 105- and 75-mm artillery used on our side but not only did these big guns get mired in the mud, but the heavy equipment required to pull these weapons forward also became stuck. Nevertheless, these two weapons along with our 40-mm anti-tank weapon caused more damage and loss of life to the Germans than they expected. And while, to the surprise of some of our troops, the Germans' 88-mm shells were easily handled and stored, they were not as much so as the 45-caliber ammunition we all carried.

We were always on the move. Most of the time we did not have cooked food and sometimes not even K-rations. We never saw the C-rations consisting of soups and meats, probably because they had to be heated and were packed in boxes too large for riflemen to carry. I weighed 180 pounds and was 5 feet, 11 inches tall just before the Normandy invasion. When I arrived home following the war, I weighed 135 pounds.

Rain, mud and bad weather slowed down the armies of the world during the summer of 1944. We lived and walked in mud throughout Europe. The ever-present mud, damp clothing and swollen streams presented a constant threat to us foot soldiers, making it difficult to keep our ammunition dry and clean. Once we became drenched with rain, we stayed wet until our body heat or the air dried our clothing. Depending on the weather, this could seem to take forever.

Everyone dreaded this war-weary trip toward Paris. But there was no place to go except forward and get the war over as fast as possible.

Our vehicles and tanks got mired in the mud on a daily and sometimes hourly basis. When we could not get the vehicles going or out of the road, we left them where they stopped. Later, when the tanks could not move out, another vehicle pushed them over the side of a bridge or into a gully just to get them out of the way so the others could go forward.

This may sound as if the army did not care about equipment but that is not true. They cared about the soldiers first, then the vehicles. Most of the soldiers said it clearly, over and over again, "If you cannot lead or follow, then get out of the way." This applied to vehicles as well as personnel.

We discarded useless weapons and ammunition immediately, while making every effort to obtain reliable weapons and ammunition to replace them. We even took weapons from dead soldiers when they appeared to be satisfactory for use.

The only items not thrown away, aside from K-rations, were K-bar knives and bayonets. These could be used without firearms and from the practice we'd had in basic training, came in handy to save our lives.

A K-bar knife looked similar to a hunting knife but had a double edge, making it sharp right out to the point. It could even be thrown effectively if the soldier had practiced this in basic training.

As we got further into the European theatre, we spent days without food or dry clothing because the supply personnel, the Red Ball Express, which supposedly delivered ammunition, food, gasoline and other supplies, did not arrive to refurnish us.

We could have purchased merchandise from various stores in France, if we could have gotten transportation to the cities. But we were not tourists, to say the least. Also, there were no restaurants or cafés around the corner and no warm beds in houses for us to use to stay dry and warm. We only carried things suitable for army or military use. If we could carry it and it was needed, there would be no objection to its possession.

After the war, we learned that the Red Ball Express personnel sold their entire load of merchandise, including their own government vehicles, to local civilians for any amount they could get regardless of the American troops' needs.

On this road to Paris, the Germans frustrated the Allied armies at St.Lo where they dug in deeply around their fortifications. The loud and fierce artillery barrages on both sides came almost to an impasse. The word was passed that we would wait for air strikes to come in to displace the Germans, who were fighting hard.

Observing from a small hill just outside St. Lo, where we had dug in our foxholes, we could keep just out of range of their rifle fire while avoiding their artillery firepower. When we heard the roar of airplanes and looked to the sky, we saw hundreds of our planes flying toward us. We were elated to see them but we had to keep down to avoid being shot.

The first bomb run was about three hundred yards short of the German fortifications. Frantic telephone calls to the rear corrected the mistake and when the bombing resumed, the German fortifications were struck. But many U.S. soldiers had been killed because of this mistake. Seeing our American soldiers blown to pieces with arms, legs and blood strewn all over the ground for many yards, saddened all of us, causing many to curse the pilots. But the improperly placed markers and the communication between the ground and aircraft was not the best.

I thought about my brother Andrew, a pilot of a B-17. With the bombing of targets in Germany and around the front lines, I wondered if he was one of those pilots.

It took about three weeks for our troops to finally conquer St.-Lo and the price was hundreds of dead and wounded. We had to move many dead soldiers' bodies at St. Lo so the vehicles could go forward. The lack of running water made it difficult to wash off the blood that got on our clothing and hands. Nevertheless, we made futile attempts using the small amount of drinking water in our canteens.

Again this shows how war is cruel and unreal especially for the soldiers in the field. Sure, the graves-registration people were supposed to be doing the job of moving the dead but there was no time to wait. At this juncture we all worked together and did what was expected as we were alive and wanted to remain that way. We wanted to ensure that our dead would not be mutilated beyond what the bombs and artillery had already done. But since the bodies lay in the roadway, the tank treads or wheels of other vehicles could crush them further.

Immediately after our Air Force devastated their army at St. Lo, the Germans began retreating toward Paris and also on the road leading to Berlin. We followed them often not knowing our location except that it was the direction in which the Germans were retreating.

Over time, our confusion increased because they retreated as fast as they could. Most units had difficulty staying in contact with the enemy or our even own troops. Moreover, the roads were not marked but they were the best routes to travel toward Berlin; so we took up the march eastward. The hedgerows finally ended just after St. Lo, which pleased us immensely.

On Toward Paris

After three days of waiting for orders from headquarters, we prepared to move east toward Paris. On the final morning, we saw a little girl about seven or eight years old standing twenty yards from our area. She did not say a word but her body and her clothing showed us that she needed food.

Unfortunately we had no cooking accommodations so all we had were the hard chocolate candy bars that came with the K-rations. Biting into these candy bars could not break them. Most men carried this candy in their pockets hoping it would become warm and chewable.

It had been three days since we received our last ration so our K-rations had all been consumed. At this point we were moving out hoping to end the war soon. I felt sympathetic toward this child, so I walked over and gave her my entire candy supply saying, "Maybe I will never need this." I am sure she did not understand but the smile she gave me was worth the effort. Since that time, I have often thought of this little girl and hoped that she did not get hurt.

We learned that the Germans agreed to fall back from Paris rather than fight for its occupation. This occurred through diplomatic proceedings, as we later learned. Naturally, the French people were extremely happy to hear the news of their capital being spared from the bombs and artillery fire. We were elated as well. We began our long trek toward Paris within days of this news.

After St. Lo, things seemed relatively uneventful for a while. We experienced little German resistance on the road to Paris except for pockets of snipers – remnants of the German army hidden in the forests that were not ready to surrender. They attempted to kill any American they observed.

We knew the German army, hoping to retard the advancement of the American troops, had laid mines on this road as their men retreated from the cities and towns. However, a special mine-sweeping tank was able to explode the mines, proving the Germans' effort to be futile. This huge tank had many chains hanging from a round bar attached to the front. This bar revolved, throwing the chains in a circle so they'd strike the ground as the vehicle moved forward detonating the mines on the roadway and in the fields. Thanks to this mine-sweeping tank, the road to Paris was not as bad as we had expected.

One day, we were pleasantly surprised when a water truck pulled into an open field near a wooded area close to us. The driver set up a large tent and started his motors. We discovered that he had set up showers for us.

What a pleasure to have clean warm water running over my body. Most of us had not experienced this good feeling for such a long time. Following the showers we received new clothing and shoes to wear, which surprised and pleased us as well.

This shower was the first we had since landing in France, about fifty or more days earlier. The next shower we had was just before entering the area of Aachen, which was about thirty-five days after that.

We got rides on trucks heading east, which felt great on our feet. The trucks carried food and supplies to the troops already in Paris. The First Infantry Division had already entered the city and we knew that somewhere nearby the 29th Infantry Division Headquarters was setting up communications for a short stay.

Happy people filled the streets of Paris when we arrived. Wine flowed like a river. When we settled down in a happy mood ourselves, we decided to visit Notre Dame Catholic Church while we had the chance. We had no idea when or if we would ever return. We walked to the church because we could see the steeple from our location. It took only a few minutes to get there. We were amazed at the beauty and the construction.

We walked anywhere we pleased because the French citizens were so happy to see us and to show us a good time. A wine merchant invited us to his vineyard to see how the wine was stored and made.

It is difficult to explain how huge this building was. Wood stanchions, apparently of oak about five or six inches in circumference, held the roof and sides together in various places. The hogsheads of wine, at least twenty feet high and almost as wide, labeled to identify the contents, continued for row after row throughout the large building. Of course, we had to taste certain ones at the insistence of our host.

When we prepared to depart, our host directed us to the subways, about a thirty-minute ride from the vineyard to the center of our group command post. It seems hilarious today, thinking back on the picture of us soldiers riding the subway loaded down with weapons, ammunition, and bottles of wine. No one commented about our appearance and we did not damage any property or offend anyone on our way to rejoin our group.

When we departed the subway train, we were invited into a building. I did not know it was a house for call girls until we arrived inside. Again, we were surprised because we saw women dressed in very little if any clothing.

When I sat down, a girl came over and placed her hand between my legs. She squeezed so hard and hurt me so badly that I had to decline all of her advances and leave the building because of the pain. Some of the guys laughed at me as I hobbled unsteadily from the building with tears in my eyes.

As normal for the military, time was against us and all good things had to come to an abrupt end. We moved out within twenty-four hours, headed toward Aachen, Germany. The map that the CO gave us included directions and instructions.

We did not know the exact location of the Division Headquarters. Some might ask how we could find our way if we had to deliver a message to them? The answer is that information always came down to the troops. Orders were received on field telephones assigned to the officer in charge who kept all maps and messages.

In December prior to Christmas, I received a letter from my brother Maurice informing me that he was located in Antwerp, Belgium with an anti-aircraft (AA) outfit. I had not seen him in almost two years.

I obtained permission to travel to see him. I personally received maps from the commanding officer showing our route from our present position toward Berlin. He told me to guard the maps because they contained information about troop movement. I would be on my own to get transportation to Antwerp.

It was easy to follow the road maps that we had of Europe. At that time military trucks were traveling the roads as fast as they could to deliver ammunition, gasoline and above all, K-rations. (At times they had C-rations available, but I never saw any.) I got three rides heading toward my destination in Antwerp. I let the truck drivers know how much I appreciated these. When the driver of the third truck let me out, he informed me where I could locate the headquarters of the AA outfit.

I began to hitchhike again as I still had a few miles to travel. The very next truck coming along stopped to give me a ride. When the driver yelled at me, I realized it was my brother Maurice. We both were surprised. He asked me where I going and of course I said to see him.

We had a very nice visit including a detailed discussion of our family. He took me to his mess hall where I received my first hot meal in about two months. Finally, the hours caught up with us and we were forced to go to bed. He gave me a bunk that one of his men prepared for me in the same tent with him.

As usual, I never got much sleep because the buzz bombs, as we called them, kept up their awful noise all night. The anti-aircraft guns kept firing at them shooting most of them down before they crossed the channel into England. A fuel contained in the cylinder propelled the V-2 rockets and also housed the explosives that were set off on impact.

The next morning, my brother got a jeep from the motor pool and gave me a ride back toward Aachen, which was about forty miles or more. Before we got to Aachen, we noticed an Army truck and waved it down. I asked the driver to give me a ride, said goodbye to my brother and climbed aboard the truck.

When I arrived back at the staging area I had left the day before, my group had moved out. Later the next day, I caught up with them by asking directions of other soldiers and using the maps given to me by the CO.

I finally reported to the unit well after dark. I did not know the password, which had changed as it usually did. But one of the guards who knew me recognized my voice and allowed me to enter the perimeter where I finally located a place to lie down to try to sleep. Otherwise I would have been sleeping away from the unit and the people I knew subjecting myself to enemy firepower.

About this time, the CO determined that I was the only one who could drive a vehicle in the entire unit of about twenty people. Most of the men were from New York or New Jersey and had not learned to drive. Therefore the CO selected me to go to Bonn, Germany to pick up a German automobile that a tank unit commander had located and was holding for him there.

With maps I'd received showing where the enemy would most likely be stationed and where I should find my unit when I returned, I hitchhiked on military vehicles to Bonn.

My travel was not direct but wound around several enemy strongholds. Armed with my maps, I directed each of my volunteer drivers on the proper roads to travel. When I arrived in Bonn it only took a few hours to locate the tank battalion.

By this time it was getting dark and fearing I'd get lost, I decided to remain overnight. The tank battalion commander, learning I had not eaten, requested that I be fed and also furnished me a place to sleep under one of the tanks after informing me that I would get used to the tanks idling all night.

They never turned the motors off to make sure they were ready to run in a moment's notice. However, because of guns firing all around us, I was awake most of the night anyhow. Early the next morning, I had coffee and a K-ration. Then I picked up the vehicle designated for my CO and started back toward my destination.

After about an hour on the road, the engine became hot. I noticed a farmhouse off the road and turned in to get water to cool the engine. The farmer attempted to talk to me but I did not speak German or French.

He kept pointing toward an area in the direction I was traveling. He tried to persuade me, by pointing in the direction from which I had come, to turn around and return to the tanks. I thanked him for the water and drove on toward my destination without understanding what he had said.

But about a mile from his farmhouse it dawned on me what he had been trying to say. To my surprise, I came upon a German tiger tank partially hidden off the main road. The thought that the power of the tank and its guns could blow me to pieces scared me so much I could hardly think.

I chose the only way I knew of getting around the ugly mess. I pretended nothing was wrong and continued to drive forward without reducing my speed.

As it turned out, the reasoning I used was sound. To my complete relief, I avoided being blown apart. As I figured, the tank commander would not reveal himself due to the dangers of aircraft fire. So I kept up the pace for about a mile or more.

I saw no signs to identify the roads, so I counted the small roads that intersected the road I was traveling on. With my usual luck, when I returned to where I'd left my unit, no one was in sight.

I kept going until I recognized a U.S. military person who directed me toward my battalion and unit, about ten miles east of the area. When I finally arrived there, I turned the car over to the commanding officer. I told him what kind of trouble I had experienced with it. I did not have to tell him about the tiger tank because he already knew from messages he received that the tank had been destroyed within the past hour by our aircraft.

Battle of the Bulge

When we approached the Maginot line on the border of Germany and Belgium, we encountered round dome emplacements built by the Germans. Though constructed of steel about one-inch thick, they were no match for our 40-mm anti-tank weapons. Some emplacements were cracked with large holes blown in them. We stopped long enough to inspect the inside of one and discovered German soldiers blown to pieces with only parts of their bodies visible.

The emplacements were constructed with a sheer drop of about twenty feet on the rear side known as tank traps because a tank driving over one would not survive that kind of fall. Our tank drivers had to be careful to drive where they knew their vehicle would be safe, which meant knocking out enemy tanks to protect the infantry.

The Germans had built tank traps almost everywhere. These were diamond- or triangle-shaped blocks of concrete spaced about four feet apart at the ground, making it impossible for a tank to traverse without stopping or exposing its underside to gunfire or explosives.

If the tank were exposed, the artillery, mortars or anti-tank guns would immobilize it immediately. We learned this from our experience in the hedgerows and the concrete emplacements the Germans built. These traps again faced us when we arrived near Aachen.

While in Aachen, we took cover in two barracks used by the German officers for training. These two barracks buildings were not safe by any means. However it was a roof over our heads for the first time since landing in France.

The weather was beginning to turn colder, with snow and sleet falling. Nevertheless, the weather did not halt "Bedcheck Charlie" from flying over our area attempting to photograph movements of our troops. We had orders not to shoot at him because it would reveal our location.

We only stayed at this area near the forest for two or three nights. We knew the Germans had it under their surveillance from the air as well as targeted by their artillery.

As a result of our aircraft and artillery firing ahead of the ground troops, the houses and apartments in the city near our training area were in shambles.

One day as we were checking out some of the buildings in the city, we heard a loud roar. It sounded as if a broken-down machine had erupted and the motor was trying to catch up with the front end. I admit it petrified me because this was a different type of sound than I had been hearing. When I looked up just over the building I noticed a jet aircraft flying overhead. This was the first jet airplane I had ever seen.

I am sure it was an attempt to scare the U.S. troops because it did not fire at us as it flew overhead. Some of us speculated on what the Germans would be trying next. We had no idea that they were so far along with the production of jet aircraft. However we never lost confidence in ourselves and above all we knew that the United States and not the Germans would win the war.

As we continued searching within about a block of our staging area, we located a thick metal door apparently locked from the inside. Naturally, this caused us some concern and we made every effort to break it down using metal bars and other objects lying around on the ground. We were unable to use explosives because that would pinpoint our location.

We finally broke the door open with simple tools. Inside we found many cases of liquor and wine but no people. Quite a few of the guys began to drink the contents until all of it was gone. We did not want to carry any bottles with us nor did we want anyone to know that we had the wine and liquor.

Two nights later, I remember standing guard with two other soldiers on the road near the main entrance to the compound we occupied. Our positions were far apart but we could still see each other. This night was extremely cold. Heavy snow fell and began to stick on the ground but we remained on guard duty regardless of the fact that we were cold and tired.

We tried to keep warm by huddling under blankets that we had and also by standing as close to the building as possible. Suddenly without any warning, I heard a loud snap. Almost immediately the entire area lit up by the flares dropped by "Bedcheck Charlie."

I did not move, as I'd been taught. But I knew that the pilot had seen my shadow at the entrance of the area, especially if he had made comparison photographs on an earlier night. Aircraft that dropped flares usually had cameras to take pictures of the ground below. Technicians would inspect them and notice our shapes in the photos, even if we did not move around.

The flare came down within a few feet of where I had taken my post to guard the entrance. When I reported the incident, following the departure of the aircraft, it was decided that we should move out from the area.

The next time we might not hear the snap of a flare but would hear and feel a bomb exploding around us. Obviously the surveillance crew knew about the buildings. They expected our troops to want to be inside out of the cold weather where we could stay dry and warm.

The next day, we packed up our few articles of personal gear, ammunition and weapons and finally began our departure in the late morning hours of December 24, 1944.

The weather turned colder as the snow began to fall more heavily accumulating on the ground. It was a heavy storm. The temperature fell below zero in a strong wind making it difficult to find our way going east to Berlin. The wind-blown snow began to accumulate in high mounds as if we needed somewhere to conceal ourselves in the blizzard.

We intensified our pace toward Bastone. Several trucks going in our direction slid over the ice and snow.

We heard later that the Germans bombed the entire complex that we had just left, flattening it completely. We did not know until later that the Germans had begun an offensive to drive to the North Sea killing or shooting everything in sight. That explained the bombing because the Battle of the Bulge had just begun.

As we traveled toward Bastone, we entered into the Huertgen Forest where the snow and ice became almost two feet deep. We struggled to carry our personal gear forward at a slow and treacherous pace and only when the shelling or gunfire stopped. There were no warm, dry places available that we could use to sleep or rest. If we could sleep at all, we slept on the frozen ground.

The rain, sleet, ice and low-hanging fog prohibited the movement of vehicles on the ground as well as aircraft flying overhead to protect us from the artillery fire. Besides, the trees were too close and dense for vehicles to move through them. The area was spooky and the land was not just hilly; it had deep ditches almost everywhere. We could barely see due to the weather, the closeness of the trees and the hilly terrain.

Our patrols that went out looking to find the Germans were in deep trouble not only because of the snow and ice but because the frozen ground crunched under their feet as they walked. This notified anyone within hearing distance that troops were moving nearby.

In addition to this, the dense forest prohibited most soldiers from seeing ahead of them to ensure they were not walking into a trap. The movement was slow and the sounds were magnified many times making us realize that talking or any other noise we made was dangerous. Our objective was to locate the enemy, determine how many there were but not to engage them in a gunfight because the information about their location was more important than the fight at that time.

As we continued moving into the Huertgen Forest, we encountered a more severe snowstorm that began about two in the afternoon. By the time it got dark around four, the snow was almost two feet deeper and marching was difficult.

We kept walking on the ice and snow until about eight that night and then we dug in for a long night of shelling and gunfire. The temperature was hovering around minus ten degrees. It was so cold that we could not move without pain. We could not build fires nor was there any heat source for a person to get warm even just a little. We could not walk, lie down or even sit because the body would not respond. Our joints were so stiff we had difficulty avoiding being hit by German artillery.

I have never been so cold in my life as in the forest outside of Aachen and hope that I never get that cold again. Ever since then, I have suffered chills and cold almost all the time. As an example my wife, Dottie, does not use many blankets at night and insists on raising the windows regardless of the temperature outside. For me, this is freezing and I must get additional blankets to stay warm.

We had a blanket, a sleeping bag and the clothes we were wearing to keep warm the best we could under the severe weather conditions. Along with limited ammunition and rifles, these were all we had. There was no food, water or a dry place to lie down.

We attempted to dig holes in the ground to protect our bodies from the bursting shells that kept coming in toward our position. The digging in was not easy because there was no dirt. It was just ice, snow, and pieces of frozen wood from the surrounding trees.

We learned the hard way that Bastone was the last strong defense that the Germans had and they used it every way they could to stop us from getting to Berlin and forcing them to surrender. On one occasion at Malmedy, a squad of U.S. paratroopers attempted to surround the Germans but the SS immediately surrounded them.

The paratroopers agreed to surrender by turning in all of their weapons as ordered by their captors. Then they were herded together and shot with machine gun fire. Fortunately, one of the men survived this ordeal to report the sad situation of how the brave U.S. paratroopers fought to the end.

This type of action by the Germans was typical of cowards and still prevails today in a world of terrorists who gun down those who are helpless. Our German prisoners said that they were instructed not to take prisoners but to get to the North Sea by any means possible.

The German soldiers took the clothes from the dead U.S. soldiers and dressed as Americans. A few days later, about ten kilometers from Malmedy, our guards captured some German soldiers wandering around the woods dressed as Americans.

These men admitted they had shot the American soldiers at Malmedy.

One sure question used to identify a German was to ask the World Series winner. When they could not give the correct answer, they were killed or captured on the spot. Once we learned of the massacre at Malmedy, there was no sympathy toward any German.

Later, a battalion of U.S. soldiers made an area into a Prisoner of War (POW) camp. After a few days, we had three camps completely full of German soldiers. Although I was not connected to the POW camp, near the end of the war I took great pleasure, when the opportunity presented itself, to escort a number of the captured soldiers into the camp.

We ground troops could not move forward because the sky was overcast and had been that way for several weeks. This kept the aircraft from flying to cover us. The foot soldiers could be effective if they could move about on the ground but in Bastone the ground was frozen solid and all our vehicles, including the tanks, were out of gasoline.

Even though we escaped injury or death due to the cold, it was impossible to dig in or get a hole to cover ourselves from enemy firepower. We sought cover under or behind anything that could offer protection, even hugging the trees to escape the falling shells.

During this time in the Huertgen Forest, there was constant artillery firing. We were at the mercy of the German artillery and we had very little or no ammunition for rifles or mortars. Even some of the bazooka teams had no ammunition to fire at the oncoming German tanks.

Almost every minute, the shells would hit the top of the trees and the flying shrapnel would make a singing sound, scattering to the ground below. We could not see the pieces falling but we could hear the whistle as they fell toward us. Therefore, we stood as close to the trees as possible to keep from getting hit by these pieces. Some soldiers, including me, carried shrapnel in our bodies for years after the war.

Thankfully, because units of the 3rd Armored Division eventually got gasoline and moved forward, we are alive today. Even in the snow and the frozen ice, which measured about three feet at that time, the tanks made it through to keep us alive.

One night during the barrage of artillery firing, I heard the thump of the 88s as usual and the next thing I knew, I awoke just prior to daybreak lying in a frozen ditch. To this day I do not know what happened but on awakening I realized that I was frozen to the ground.

I was aware that some of the guys were trying to release my feet from the ditch. I could not think straight and had no idea where I was or what I was doing in this hellhole. I could not move. My entire body and clothing were frozen to the ground as if by glue and I could not get up.

Some of the guys who were trying to get me on my feet said I had been there most of the night. They wanted to take me to the medical aid station to see a doctor but they could not get me awake or on my feet.

Three guys worked to free me and finally they got me to a medic. The examination revealed nothing of importance to the medic and he could not determine why I was in such pain.

About two weeks later following the pullback of the Germans, a doctor examined me because I could not move very well and continued to feel pain. He was a pediatrician who had joined the Army some weeks earlier, arriving in Bastone just prior to the Germans' push toward the North Sea.

He said his examination revealed nothing serious, no wounds or injuries of any kind. He gave me some APC or aspirin tablets for pain and instructed me to return to full duty.

My back and legs hurt so badly that I could have cried but the medication eased the pain to a degree. I kept trying to get back on my feet and take care of myself. Because we were in the forest, the uneven ground made it difficult to walk. I eventually became mobile and began to walk but only at a staggering gait. I had even more difficulty when lying down. I kept trying to find a comfortable position, but this turned out to be impossible.

During all of my tour In Europe and even before we entered Germany, I kept asking the medic for APC tablets, which contained Phenobarbital, to ease my headaches, which were so bad that I became nauseated, leading me to believe I suffered from migraines. A physician later confirmed this before I departed Germany. However, none of this was recorded in my medical record.

After being frozen to the ground, I requested medication not only for my headaches but also for my lower back, which continued in constant pain, especially when I was cold. The only relief I received for the lower back pain was the APC pills dispensed by the medic.

There was no doctor present in the unit with us, and since the war was winding down, they saw no need to try anything different for me. All doctors and medics informed me to contact the Veterans Administration (VA) when I arrived back in the States.

The Germans had penetrated the British flank and were driving toward the North Sea. This in effect cut us off from any help or relief from American forces. Had the weather remained the way it had been for another week we may all have been captured, maybe killed.

One night after we had pushed the Germans back, I was standing guard. It was near midnight when I heard movement in the bushes on a hill above me. I pulled the chamber of my M-1 open to insert a round of ammunition in the barrel because I believed the noise was coming from German soldiers beginning another attack. The night was still with no wind and the opening of the chamber on the M-1 made a lot of noise that could be heard at a long distance.

As I prepared to fire, this voice called out, "Don't shoot." I recognized it as one of our men. He had departed the area without telling us to go to the bathroom in the woods. For this he was soundly warned.

Throughout this time, every soldier was needed to defend the area as best he could with very little or no ammunition. Even though we experienced the artillery shells and noise from mortars and other weapons, we did not know we were completely surrounded by the Germans and did not consider ourselves prisoners by any means.

Then the German Command sent a group of soldiers under a flag of truce to speak with General Tony McAuliffe, who was the Commander of the Second Army. The German soldiers were ordered to wear blindfolds and were escorted to the general's area, a makeshift tent where they presented their demands.

We all remember what he said to the Germans when they requested that he surrender all forces under his command. With one word he said it clearly and precisely, "Nuts," to their demands to surrender. We all applauded his answer and even though we had very little ammunition and practically no food, we admired him immensely.

Some officers serving under General McAuliffe wanted to shoot the truce team because of the Malmedy incident but he would have no part of this type of activity. Following this truce team's departure, we all banded together for the drive, which we knew was coming.

It started out with shelling. Then the tanks began to roll toward our positions, shooting everything in the path of the guns. However, we knew the Germans were just as cold and frozen as we were and that they wanted to get the war over too.

We were placed in a defensive position with no place to go except to try to push forward with limited ammunition and little motorized equipment, most of which was parked at different places because there was no fuel supply.

We allowed the Germans to go forward while inflicting many casualties on them. They apparently had plenty of ammunition, which they used indiscriminately, attempting to frighten us to surrender. This did not work because we were so close to the end of the war, we would not give up.

We were thankful when the sun finally appeared one morning, after three weeks of clouds had kept our aircraft grounded. It was a glorious sight. We all cheered, happy to put the three weeks of snow, ice and fog behind us. The U.S. aircraft flew overhead strafing and bombing the German tanks and their positions.

At the same time, our tanks and armored units arrived with their guns blasting the German tanks and other vehicles out of the way. Their support helped us soldiers move out of our pockets where we had nowhere to turn and gave everyone an opportunity to move toward Cologne. Eventually this led us to Halle, Germany on the road to Berlin and the winding-down of the hostilities.

German Surrender and Homeward Bound

As we approached Berlin, across the Rhine River stood a beautiful cathedral, hardly touched by the bombs. We had little time to look at this beautiful building. We were reminded that we were in a war and not on a sightseeing trip. But what I saw of the massive structure thrilled me.

In April, we received the information that Hitler had committed suicide and that the Russians had linked up with the 69th Division near Halle, a short distance from Cologne making the surrender of Germany imminent. The Russian army pushed into Berlin, burning and shooting everything in sight. The German army had no place to go. Their only option was complete surrender by the hundreds and eventually by the thousands.

The Germans chose to surrender to the Americans. Thousands upon thousands of German soldiers were herded into compounds with barbed wire fencing. We were elated, realizing that we could begin thinking of going home.

Most of the U.S. soldiers had accumulated points by virtue of their time in the service and doing overseas duty. We began to count the earned credits to calculate our turn to be rotated back to the U. S. in accordance with the regulations we received prior to going overseas. Then with the German army surrendering in droves, we learned that within a few weeks we would be on our way back to the good old U.S. of A.

Personally, I was ready to leave German soil and the war with all of its dirt, mud and rain, particularly after the incident when I froze to the ground while in the ditch in Bastone, not to mention the constant shelling by the German artillery. I stated my comments loudly to anyone who would listen that I wanted to go home because I had enough of the war and its deprivations.

By this time the German army had surrendered unconditionally, which made it easier for most of us to prepare to go home. The Colonel asked me to go to the Far East and serve in the Army with any battalion or company I chose. I said, "No thanks." I did not want to make the army a career and also my aches and pains were getting worse. With the Colonel's blessing, I made preparations to depart for home.

Prior to my departure, I talked with a physician at a higher level who insisted that I have a knee operation just as soon as I arrived in the U.S. He urged me to consult with my family doctor and to get a second opinion regarding the headaches.

He expressed this urgency in words for which I will forever be grateful. He also stated that I should have a physician carefully examine my back, which had begun to cause me severe pain when I walked or stood for long periods of time. Following his examination he informed me that X-rays showed I might lose my leg if special care was not taken because the badly bruised knee joint contained a tumor.

I did not know it then but none of these recommendations was written in my medical record. In fact no physician wrote any medical opinions regarding my pains or injuries, an omission that has haunted me ever since.

Within a two-week period we received orders to depart by truck to Antwerp to board a ship to return to the U.S. We made haste turning in our weapons and other equipment preparing to travel to Antwerp.

When our convoy arrived at the port of Antwerp, we joined additional troops from many divisions to board a victory ship for the return trip home. Naturally we felt happy to be going back to the greatest country in the world.

We went aboard the ship and found our way to bunks and dry places to sleep – an anomaly to all of us. The ship was delayed for a few days in port, which allowed the clerks time to compute our pay and attempt to get our records straight. We had not gotten paid for at least three months although we had no place to spend the money.

Prior to our departure, the Red Cross workers, who stood on the piers outside of the gangplank, served us coffee and doughnuts. Finally everything was completed and the order was issued to board the ship. We set sail the following morning.

The entire voyage from Antwerp until the ship docked in New York was again extremely bad for me. I was seasick the entire time, repeating my experience on the trip to Scotland. However this time none of us were assigned extra duties in the galleys or other parts of the ship. We just plain loafed around the ship. Some of the men played cards and won money; others lost their shirts.

The trip back to the States was a few days shorter than the one going over to Scotland. We arrived in New York and eventually took the train to Fort Dix, New Jersey. There we were processed out of the military.

It took almost a week to record each soldier's history. Like most of the other soldiers, I was so anxious to get home that I made the mistake of skipping over the answers to many important questions regarding pains and hurts I suffered while in Europe. We were not knowledgeable of the paperwork and believed the Veterans Administration (VA) would research our records and provide the necessary treatment.

But as most of us learned later, since we did not take the time to have many illnesses and diseases recorded, the VA apparently took this as an excuse to not treat us for them. Because I failed to tell the doctors many things that I assumed were already in my medical record, the Veterans Administration later disallowed many of my complaints, stating the VA doctors could not treat me. Much to my sorrow, the subsequent medical treatment denied by the VA included treating the pains I suffered in Bastone.

The processors finally decided that I was eligible to return to civilian life. I felt so happy to be back in the grand country of the United States of America. I could hardly wait to get home to Vinton.

While in Germany, a small bright spot entered my life after we moved forward from Belgium. I noticed a small puppy following me and the other guys looking for food. I decided to feed the dog and it began to follow me wherever I went. I named the puppy Schnappsy after a German whiskey

The dog reminded me of a fox. She was with me and the other guys most of the time and we enjoyed her company. On cold nights, especially when we were in Bastone, she would sleep at the bottom of my sleeping bag, which helped me stay somewhat warm in the freezing temperatures. Schnappsy could smell or hear a German soldier prior to his arrival. She would growl very low, as if she knew that loud noise was not appropriate under these circumstances.

Naturally, I did not want to abandon this little dog so I secretly carried her aboard ship and down into the hold to our sleeping quarters, knowing she would be safe even though it was damp down there. Once a day, I took her food from my plate, as there was nothing else I could feed her.

Upon our arrival in New York, I carried the dog down the gangplank as if she belonged to the ship or the captain and nobody questioned me. I found a civilian worker and imposed upon him to build me a wooden cage so the dog would not get hurt when I shipped her to my mother's home in Vinton.

He not only made the box; he assisted me in getting her shipped after I paid the freight. Later I learned from my mother that Schnappsy growled at everybody prior to being released from the box. I also discovered once I arrived home that she'd given birth to four puppies. Maybe this was why she was so cantankerous toward everyone.

She became pregnant because one of my buddies did not watch her after I told him she appeared to be in heat. When I returned to the compound I learned she and a male dog had gotten together. There was nothing I could do at that time.

I wrote to my mother after I got to Ft. Dix. My letter arrived ahead of me, giving her an opportunity to prepare. She notified her family members and others who might want to know of my return.

Schnappsy lived with my mother for about six years. Finally, when I was in college, my mother wrote to tell me she had died.

Service men going home from the war packed the train headed toward West Virginia and places further west. When we departed Fort Dix, at least a dozen other soldiers took the train to Roanoke. Others got off at various other places.

We had a wonderful time talking, discussing our plans for the future and what had happened in Europe. We received the "ruptured duck," indicating our release from the military and the entire WW II affair. We all were elated to be headed home, away from the misery we encountered at almost every turn during the war, the filthy conditions and especially the rain, mud and lack of warm places to sleep or eat. The consensus was that the military service was not in our future. In fact, most men stated they would probably not join the reserves.

We also discussed the lack of facilities where a soldier could vacate his bowels without being shot by an enemy soldier. What did we do for these necessary things of life? What I did was find a bush or low place in the ground making sure to cover up the evidence with dirt after I finished.

The train made a stop at Bedford, Virginia, about thirty miles from Roanoke, to release several soldiers. We knew that many men from Bedford had perished at Normandy and we were sad for those who did not make it back. At the same time, we were pleased, honored and happy to be going home to our loved ones – mixed feelings difficult to describe.

During the fall of 1999, Dottie and I visited the site in Bedford where a memorial was to be built to honor those men who gave their lives at Normandy. The 29th Infantry Division led the way by storming the shores of France on Omaha Beach. They were chosen to lead the invasion of the greatest army in the world. May God rest their souls and keep them warm and dry.

Once I arrived home, I talked about Europe to my family, describing the places, countries and people I had seen. I felt proud telling my family of these places and what little we saw, since this was not a sightseeing tour. I did not describe some of the horrors I had experienced or the scares that were thrown upon me.

I recall that my uncle Lewis Roop, a deaf mute, traveled from Blacksburg to see and welcome me home. This really pleased me because of the effort he made.

After I was home for about two weeks, I informed my parents that I would travel to Macon to talk with Marie Deery whom I had left almost three years earlier before departing for Europe. I took the bus because the bus station was near their home.

The tiring trip on that slow bus took almost twelve hours. After telephoning Marie's family, I arrived at their home where I was received politely and graciously. But I became aware of a new atmosphere, different from the one prior to my leaving to go overseas. Marie had changed in her mannerisms and her thoughts were more on material things than I had noticed three years earlier. We had only one day to talk because she was still working at the local bank and could get very few hours to spend with me.

Marie had wanted me to visit her prior to going to Vinton following my return from the war. In her opinion, she came before my parents. I was not prepared to accept that premise. After I told her of my pending operations and how I had pains in other parts of my body, she showed little interest in me for a long-term relationship.

She continued to question me about my plans for employment and living arrangements. I promised that I would write and inform her of the operations as well as my attempts to get employment. I also told her that I was trying to save funds to purchase an automobile that would allow me the pleasure of driving to visit her when my health improved.

I told her that I planned to go to college and complete my education. I was especially interested in getting my operations over before I made any final plans or commitments.

Within a period of six months, I stopped getting letters from her except for one in which she wrote that she had become engaged and was planning to marry. I did not know the person to whom she was engaged and I have no knowledge of her whereabouts today.

PART 3 THE VETERANS ADMINISTRATION (VA) AND WAR-RELATED INJURIES

More Surgery

When I returned to Vinton from my visit with Marie, I decided it was time to visit the physician to get a diagnosis on my knee and my back. I secured an appointment with Dr. Hoover, the same orthopedic surgeon who had set my broken arm years earlier.

After he made an examination, he advised me to consult with one of the VA physicians in Salem, Virginia, as I needed an operation on my left knee as soon as possible. He telephoned one of the physicians at the VA and secured an appointment for me.

At the hospital in Salem, I informed the physician of my visit with Dr. Hoover. The VA physician referred me to the Woodrow Wilson Army Hospital in Staunton, Virginia, and said he would write them a letter after which I would have to deal with them directly.

In April 1946, I was admitted to Woodrow Wilson Hospital for the operation. I remained there for about two weeks. I had to learn to walk again and take therapy for another week until I was released back to VA care.

I was referred back to the VA Hospital in Salem for follow-up treatment, which lasted about a month but therapy was not offered. Excuses and delaying tactics were the order of the day.

My slow recovery was very tiring and painful especially when I walked or exercised to recover my strength. After two months of exercising on my own, I decided to obtain employment thinking that working would be the same as walking.

I could not return to the iron works employment because of my knees and back condition. But with the assistance of the VA, I found employment at a floor-finishing company, selling and demonstrating their machines. I believed that my employment with this company would be stable so I exerted myself in order to please my employer.

As the months passed, I began to have pain in my knee again, which hampered me in bending or lifting most of the heavy sanding machines. I informed my boss, stating that I might have to get an opinion from the surgeon as to the cause. He allowed me sufficient time to consult with the doctor during my working hours; however he voiced a cautionary opinion that I was not entitled to long periods of time off.

Within a year following the first operation, I began getting very sharp pains that interfered with walking, causing me to limp with each step. At no time did I stay away from work because of my pain. However, it felt excruciating most of the time.

When I visited the doctor at the VA within a month of my years' employment, he stated that I must have another operation. The VA doctor contacted Dr. Hoover to set a date for him to operate on my knee. In fact he requested through the VA representative that I visit his office for an in-depth examination prior to the operation.

Dr. Hoover examined my knee, made the necessary X-rays and agreed that I had to have another operation on the same knee. He explained that he now had been hired to perform these operations at the VA Hospital in Salem, Virginia.

Following the operation in April 1947, Dr. Hoover informed me that he had found some foreign matter in my knee joint, which he removed. He suggested that the knee would get better over a period of time. However I would continue to be in pain because arthritis in the joint would cause me more suffering.

I stayed in the hospital about three weeks, receiving therapy daily. In about two months, the surgeon finally discharged me from his care. During this stay in the VA Hospital in Salem, I informed the doctors about my back pain. Whenever I moved, it felt as if my bones were breaking. I informed them that sleeping on my back was the only way I could rest. I told them how it hurt, where it hurt and what help I needed to move or get out of bed.

My description of the cold, wet and frozen conditions in Bastone did not make an impression on any of the doctors. They told me that I had a strain and after bed rest my back would be fine.

The surgeon stated that my knee should come first. Then I could discuss my back condition at a later date.

When the VA doctors came around to see me, I also explained that about every three to four months my ear passages would fill with fluid so that I could not hear anything. These doctors paid no attention to my complaints and never made a record of them.

Following my discharge from the VA Hospital, I bought a syringe to rinse out my ear passages. This helped me for a few weeks. Finally an ear specialist began a treatment that lasted for almost six months. This included rinsing out my ears and then pushing medication into the canals.

This treatment was satisfactory and I began to regularly rinse my own ears about every six months. Since that time, except for an occasional flare-up when I have to visit a doctor for additional treatment, I have gotten along quite well treating myself.

One of those flare-ups occurred after I obtained a job in Norfolk, Virginia when I experienced hearing loss. I found an ear doctor who treated me for almost six months, trying to improve my hearing. The VA did not cover this expense, as the hearing loss was not considered a result of my military service. In fact, all funds for these treatments came from my personal account. At no time did the doctors say that the sounds of guns firing while I was in the military had any effect on my hearing.

While I was a patient in the VA Hospital in Salem, my employer demanded a reason why I was not able to report to work. He needed me to work jobs he had contracted to be completed in a specified time. When he learned that I would be absent for another month as a result of my disability, he informed my mother that I did not have a job with his company because he considered me an undependable employee.

Our family had always been dedicated to the work ethic and upon my release from the VA Hospital, I sought employment at various business places because I wanted to get a reliable job for my future. I acquired this attitude as a younger person living through our family's dire straits. I have always had a drive to get ahead through honest employment.

My oldest brother, Maurice applied for a position with the Roanoke Fire Department and was hired. He worked as a fireman until he retired with the rank of captain. He subsequently passed away in February 2001.

My brother Andrew, after his release from the Air Force, had been rehired at his old job with an insurance company. Through him I learned of a possible opening at a local bank, where his boss knew most of the officers. He agreed to talk with his boss to find out if I could get a job there.

I learned in discussions with Andrew that in 1944, he flew one of the heavy B-17 aircraft over St. Lo, bombing Germany. He said he thought of me as he was flying over the Alps toward his targets and wondered where I was at that time.

Since that time we have discussed many topics but we have stayed clear of the war as much as possible. He did brag to me about the expertise of his navigator who even though he drank gin and grapefruit juice continuously while in the air, could be relied upon to bring him home every time. Andrew died in September 2004.

As he promised, Andrew discussed my condition with his boss at the insurance company. Andrew's boss was a personal friend of the vice president at the First National Exchange Bank in Roanoke. Following an interview, I was hired as a bookkeeper operating a machine, which posted customers' accounts. Although I took the job, this routine work was not for me because it presented no challenge. It made me think about my future and some of the things I really wanted to do.

Additionally, I was assigned to teach young college graduates how the banking procedures worked and how they could best get ahead in banking. These young people had not been in the military or to war but had gone to college to get an education.

In observing them, I saw how they were promoted rapidly. In fact, one of them became my boss. This forced me to consider the best course of action for me regarding employment.

I contacted the VA regarding jobs and schooling but their assistance was limited to on-the-job training at that time and the representative refused to talk with me about further education. Obviously my training in the military did not prepare me for civilian jobs, which placed severe limits on my prospects for jobs in Roanoke.

Moreover, although wartime work was still in progress, businesses were all geared to dismantling war production and returning to local commerce. As a result of this situation, I decided to go back to school as soon as I had saved sufficient funds.

During my employment at the bank, I began to study business law and accounting at night at the Kennett School of Commerce in Roanoke thinking that it might help me in my future employment. I enjoyed the challenge of these courses. Mr. Scott, my law professor, represented a well-known and respected law office in Roanoke.

Less than fourteen months later, with the pain in my left knee having become ever-more excruciating, I again contacted Doctor Hoover, the surgeon who operated on me at the VA Hospital. Doctor Hoover made an examination of my knee and informed me that another operation was the only thing he could do to relieve the pain. Doctor Hoover performed this third operation at the VA Hospital, after which he recommended extensive therapy. Many weeks of painful therapy helped me to walk correctly.

I remained in the VA hospital almost one month, interrupting my job at the bank. With nothing else to do but think, I seriously considered going to college.

While in the hospital, I again informed the VA doctors of the severe pain in my lower back that prevented me from getting a full night's sleep. They told me again not to worry, that I had a strain and nothing would help that kind of pain except bed rest. They also cautioned me to be careful in lifting or carrying heavy items.

An additional ailment I discussed with the VA doctors was the fungus on my feet. I brought this to their attention many times, but they continued to say it would be all right if I purchased powder for athletes' foot and used it every day.

Later while living in Norfolk, I continued to have problems with my itching feet. I consulted a dermatologist and his son who had a practice together. They attempted to cure the fungus using X-Rays. For approximately two years, I kept appointments with the dermatologists. It appeared to help my itching feet to some degree.

I paid these bills from my personal funds even though I was never bothered with this type of infection prior to my military service and received consistent treatment for it while in the military. I know no reason why this was not recorded in my medical record or why the VA has declined to treat me for this infection except later, to furnish me with creams to rub on my feet. In fact the adjudication board in Roanoke declined to state this fungus was contracted while in the military.

A Chance Meeting

Eventually, I returned to the bank in Roanoke. The bank furnished lunch in their dining room on the top floor of the building at no cost to the employees. One day during lunch, my life changed immeasurably but pleasurably. A co-worker asked me to meet a friend of hers and go to a party the following weekend. I accepted and that is when I met my future wife, Dorothea M. Maynard.

Over a few months of dating – going to parties as well as out with other couples – we agreed that we were made for each other. We had a very good time whenever we went out; there were very few ugly words between us. She eventually invited me to her home in Williamson, West Virginia to spend a week of rest and relaxation following my last operation.

We discussed the trip and the necessary preparations in traveling and meeting her parents. She did not drive so I had to make sure that I could last the eight hours of driving even with rest stops. Finally, I agreed to do this.

Dottie, as she is best known, had worked at Dillard Paper Company in Roanoke as a secretary for many years and could count on two weeks vacation. I agreed to visit her home because I needed the relaxation and rest and I wanted to travel with her.

As we were planning, she described her hometown as a remote place without radio or telephone and very few stores. In fact, she implied but never stated for a fact that there was no running water or electricity.

My comment about these things lacking in the city of Williamson, West Virginia was, "Piffle berries." We continued to plan to drive to her parents' home.

On the way she mentioned some of her relatives who lived in remote places I had never visited, such as Bluefield, West Virginia. When we finally arrived in her hometown, the narrow roads made it difficult to park my car. They reminded me of alleyways rather than roads; however they were designated as streets.

Her parents' home was built on the side of a mountain with a rock wall near the roadway about fifteen feet high. The sidewalk was built on top of the rock wall. To get to their home, a person had to walk around the wall and climb the steps up to the sidewalk. These steps were a block long and could be entered from either end of the wall. Following this walk, we then went up two flights of steps from the sidewalk to their front porch. The effort strained my knees and back but I did not complain.

After I met her parents, we discussed our trip and the cities we drove through. They described the area and some of their neighbors. I informed her parents what Dottie said about the city and the surrounding area, mentioning the lack of electricity and running water. We all had a good laugh, which broke the ice in our meeting. Everything went smoothly from then on.

I met many neighbors and friends. This was the first time I had ever been to a coal-mining town and I was impressed with the people and their customs.

Naturally, her family was extremely cordial toward me. A pleasant surprise was meeting Eugene Murphy, who was stationed at Camp Wheeler with me during basic training. It seems that he'd met and married Dottie's best friend and next-door neighbor, Florence Reed.

Prior to his marriage, Gene had lived with his parents in Belfry, Kentucky just over the line between Kentucky and West Virginia. Now he worked for a mining company as supervisor. We had discussions about mining as well as other work and life in the town but we did not discuss the army or overseas deployments.

Dottie and I enjoyed a fine vacation and after about a week we returned to Roanoke. I must admit it was nice to have a wholesome and reliable person to travel with. Dottie has always been an excellent traveling companion and especially a dependable person in times of stress.

The rest and relaxation at her hometown helped me in many ways. For one thing, we saw each other in a different light and I again began to question my future. I finally realized that I was limited in what I could do as far as working was concerned. I began to explore the idea of what I could accomplish by the intense learning I would gain attending college.

We discussed my parents on our return trip to Roanoke because I was living with them at that time. They were living on a limited income, as my father was past the age of retirement and they both were not in the best of health. But they were supportive and caring, neither demanding of me nor concerned about what work I would do.

Above all my parents did not want to instruct me in what to do with my life. They had gotten along with a small amount of funds and fully believed that everything would work out just fine for me, my future wife and my brothers who had returned from the war.

When I finally introduced Dottie to my family, they were impressed. They spoke favorably of her and loved her dearly. My mother cautioned me not to be too harsh but to treat her kindly and tenderly and above all fairly. My father had a fine time teasing her on every occasion she visited our home, saying she was not as big as weasel.

Dottie and I continued dating. I told her she came all the way from Williamson to Roanoke to find me. We had fun going to movies, plays, parties and dinners with other couples or visiting friends and relatives together. We always found wholesome enjoyment in our association.

Dottie actually taught me to dance a little but this was nothing to brag about because I had two left feet when it came to dancing. We were together almost each week and sometimes every night when there was no work the following day. After over a year of dating, she met the other members of my family. Everyone seemed to get along just fine together.

We finally set the date to be married on June 21, 1949 at her hometown church in Williamson and we began getting all things prepared for that date. I am sure she and her parents discussed the marriage while we were visiting them previously but this was never discussed with me and I am just as pleased that it happened that way.

Following our marriage, we visited her family for many years during the summer months, staying for several weeks at a time.

We also visited some of her relatives who lived in Kentucky where her parents were born and raised.

Before we met, Dottie lived in Roanoke boarding with a family in the southwest section of the city so that she could live on her own. She learned of this family while attending National Business College in Roanoke where she was an honor student.

Dottie elected not to live with her sister, who lived in Roanoke with her husband and two children. Dottie required freedom and believed her living separately would be better since she was also employed and had a schedule to maintain.

Her sister and brother in-law have since passed away. The only relatives she now has in Virginia are a niece and her family living in Leesburg, Virginia with whom we have maintained a close relationship.

We had a very nice wedding. The preacher, who had known Dottie for many years, was exceptionally fond of the Willard Maynard family, as was most of the congregation of the church. We started out on love and it has continued through the years. Now in 2005, I have dearly loved every day and minute of our fifty-six years of marriage. Yes, we have had many arguments but they were never so severe as to cause a rupture in our marriage.

Following our wedding, Dottie's brother, Homer, did many things to make life difficult for me but they were not mean. We called them pranks. One was filling my hair cream bottle with rice. Another was tying my clothing in knots. After all, we lived in the same house and he could get to my things very easily. All in all it was mostly fun and we had many good laughs. He attempted to learn our destination for our honeymoon but we refused to tell him.

Today Homer lives in Centreville on the Eastern Shore of Maryland with his wife, Betty. We live in Norfolk, which is about four or five hours away but we visit once or twice each year. Homer and I are close friends and I always enjoy his company.

It was extremely hot the day we were married. The Daniel Boone Hotel in Charleston, West Virginia where we had reservations for our honeymoon was not completely air-conditioned; however we had a marvelous time. We visited many places in Charleston where I had never been before. On our return to Roanoke, Dottie continued to work for Dillard Paper Company and I continued to work at the First National Exchange Bank until I finally decided to go to college.

Following our marriage, Dottie's parents visited her sister in Roanoke and also my parents in Vinton. Our one-bedroom apartment, located on Elm Avenue in Roanoke, had very little furniture and was not large enough for visitors. Since there were grandchildren at her sister's, her parents felt more comfortable visiting them.

Dottie and I discussed my desire to go to college in great detail. She encouraged me and was extremely helpful in planning that part of our future. At this point we knew that we could move rather rapidly if the need arose, especially if we located an apartment with lower rent and the furnishings we wanted. Our apartment was hot in the summertime without air conditioning so we used a fan or two to help make life more bearable. In the winter however, the heat was delightful and above all appreciated.

It was about this time that I began to teach Dottie how to drive a car. I must admit it took a lot of patience from both of us because, unless she followed instructions, she wanted to do one thing and the car would do another.

Parallel parking by backing into a space was her most frustrating problem because she could not get the car to turn properly. Then of course, it was my fault.

During this training time I would stand outside of the car, directing her every move and she would try hard to please me. I recall one Saturday morning when I was teaching her to park. It was raining but not too hard. She kept trying until she learned to park the car in the proper space.

Almost every weekend over a period of two months we would practice parking and driving around the streets of Roanoke near where we lived. Finally without telling me, Dottie went with another tenant in the building and received her license. She was so proud of her accomplishment but thought I would be angry with her for going for her license with another person. But I was pleased that Dottie went on her own and showed me as well as everybody else she could do anything she tried and complete it satisfactorily.

In our discussions regarding our future lives with each other, I informed Dottie that I would make the living and she would make the living worthwhile, which has been an excellent arrangement.

College Student

In 1950, I applied for admission to several colleges. The College of William and Mary in Williamsburg, Virginia invited me to visit the campus for an interview. Since this was my first visit to Williamsburg, I took advantage of the opportunity to walk around, looking to determine how best we could live while there.

I must admit that I was thrilled to be in this historic location on Duke of Gloucester Street, the main thoroughfare. At one corner, the college begins at the Wren Building where the Lord Botetourt statue stands. About a mile west is situated the country's original Palace. I hoped that I would be accepted at the college and within about three or four weeks following this visit, I received an acceptance letter from the Dean of Admissions. I was elated to say the least.

During this interval, Dottie and I discussed my educational aspirations with our dear friend and my former high school teacher Virginia Goggin, who was most encouraging and supportive. We visited each other and enjoyed her as a person who must have thought about education continuously because she could talk on most any topic. Unfortunately, she passed away a few years later as a result of cancer. We both were deeply saddened to learn of her passing, which happened while I was attending college.

After I received the admission letter from the college, I agreed to enter school in February 1951, as the spring semester began. This required another trip to Williamsburg to locate living accommodations; this trip was an extreme pleasure. We still return to Williamsburg every chance we get.

We were fortunate to meet a person whom I knew when he lived in Vinton as a youth. He directed us to his landlady, Mrs. Bennett, saying that she would be glad to have us as tenants in one of her duplex apartments. We located her duplex in the rear of her house on Harrison Avenue. She offered us a room in her home until an apartment became available. We explained that only I would be living there while going to school until Dottie could join me in June 1951. I agreed to pay rent and to take all meals at restaurants or other establishments.

Mrs. Bennett was a retired nurse. Her husband was a doctor who visited the sick in the surrounding area by horse and buggy when they first came to Williamsburg. She also visited the poor families in the city and county and did what she could to help them by working with the health department prior to her retirement.

Mrs. Bennett was the most delightful lady anyone could ever expect to meet. Everyone who knew her loved her. Her pleasant attitude, along with her extension of friendship was expressed in everything she did or said. She could discuss many topics and was quite knowledgeable and most informative about Williamsburg, where she had lived for many years.

At one time, her house at the end of Harrison Avenue off Richmond Road was open to visitors for overnight stays. This street now enters into another main thoroughfare. The distance from the campus was only about two miles or less and if the weather was not bad, the walk was rather nice. I chose to walk when I could and left the automobile for Dottie to use after she joined me.

During the months from February until June, I lived alone in this one room, which I used for sleeping only. After learning my way around, I began going to the library nightly to study and review books. This became a passion for me.

Most of the time I would have my evening meal and stop by the library until closing time before I returned to my room to sleep. From some of the students I learned of a boarding house not far from the school's campus where they served lunch. The food was wholesome with all I wanted to eat for seventy-five cents.

After I tried this lunch, I decided to continue eating there until Dottie arrived. In my correspondence with her I told her about the lunch place and listed a few other places we might try for food upon her arrival.

Dottie, in a decision to reduce expenses, prevailed upon her sister to allow her to move into her house for just a few weeks. When her sister agreed, I planned weekend trips to Roanoke to get Dottie moved from the apartment to her sister's house. Then, in an attempt to accomplish two things at the same time, I would move some of our things to Williamsburg on my return trip. This type of moving and changing things around continued until the semester was over in June and Dottie joined me in Williamsburg.

For six months we lived in the one room at Mrs. Bennett's house and were extremely happy with the outlook. We looked forward to moving into the duplex apartment when it became vacant and were excited about our new venture in a new city, a new place for us to begin preparing for the future.

We loved every minute sharing this home with our landlady. We could always tell when she was up in the morning because we smelled her toast burning.

We eventually met both of Mrs. Bennett's daughters and two of her grandchildren who were quite impressive people. Her eldest daughter lived in Wyoming; the youngest lived in Orlando, Florida.

One of Mrs. Bennett's granddaughters lived with her after she enrolled at William and Mary as a student. This was almost three years later, near the time for me to graduate. Following Mrs. Bennett's death, I was offered an opportunity to buy her home on Harrison Avenue but at that time I could not afford to make the purchase and declined the offer, much to my disappointment.

I enjoyed attending William and Mary even though I had minor setbacks both academically and financially. I overcame the financial situation with several part-time jobs while concentrating on my studies.

The school year ended in June; however I enrolled in summer classes. We lived in our room, went out to eat our meals and waited to move into the duplex apartment. Dottie found a job as a secretary with Colonial Williamsburg, Inc.

Our lives were centered on my schooling and studying for classes, which began at eight o'clock two mornings a week and at nine or ten on other days. I enjoyed these classes where I learned many things that I had not considered prior to going to college.

Reading many books, making reports and getting to the library to read were a treat for me. We could not afford to buy books regardless of the price when I was at home in Vinton. When I observed the rows and rows of books in the library, I was thrilled.

It was expensive for Dottie and me to eat each meal out but in the long run we were happy with this arrangement. It paid off, making life much more exciting for us because we not only met different people in the town but had the opportunity to meet many visitors at Colonial Williamsburg.

I obtained a part-time job at the rear door of Colonial Williamsburg's administration building recording all who entered or left the building after hours. This job forced me to learn names and positions of most employees.

A few doors up the street from Mrs. Bennett's house lived the chief of police, a very fine person with many friends in town who enjoyed telling tales about him. For example once, after eight patients escaped from Eastern State Mental Hospital, he rounded up nine to take back. Everyone enjoyed telling such tales and he relished the idea of being discussed so widely.

While we were living in Mrs. Bennett's' house, Dottie became ill with a flu-like disease. Doctor Bell at the hospital believed she had pneumonia and ordered her admitted. She was slow recovering and remained in the hospital for four more days.

Of course this was an added expense but sickness is a fact of life and we came out of it very well with no after effects. In fact, she contacted Doctor Bell for some minor problems at a later date because there were very few doctors in Williamsburg at that time who would treat new patients.

When we finally moved into the duplex apartment, Mrs. Bennett visited us infrequently. However we were so impressed with her that we visited in her home every chance we could.

Dottie's job with Colonial Williamsburg kept her quite busy. I applied for part-time work there and was hired in the Architectural Department after school hours and at times when I could work during the days. My duties were confined to making copies of blueprints for construction purposes and filing them in the proper section. Colonial Williamsburg architects searched continuously for foundations of old buildings and needed blueprints to re-build them as they were originally.

I secured a job at the post office for Christmas, which was a great help in lowering our accumulating debts. As a result of this job, the postmaster hired Dottie. A phenomenal secretary in every respect, she was more satisfied with that position than with her job at Colonial Williamsburg.

Almost everyone in the city knew the postmaster. He was a very interesting, extremely capable, jolly person who loved a good time, regardless of the location. According to what he told me, each year he would get together with a number of older persons he associated with in Williamsburg. They would drive to Nags Head, North Carolina for a few drinks and pranks on each other.

Dottie and I kept in contact with him until he passed away. We knew that he was quite fond of Dottie and had many kind remarks to make about her as a secretary prior to his retirement.

He also helped me while she was working at the post office. I recall one time he needed the postal boxes on the street painted and offered me the opportunity to submit a bid for the entire job, knowing that I needed the funds to pay some bills. He furnished the papers and assisted me in submitting the bid. I got the job and then, with the postmaster's knowledge, hired another student to paint for a lesser amount of money.

My studies required me to make every day and almost all hours count. However, when I found myself in absolute need of funds, I went to the golf course to caddy for some of the players – generally tourists staying at the Williamsburg Inn.

I met and became friends with the golf professional, Jimmy Weeks. Because I assisted him at the clubhouse, he allowed me to play golf at times without paying the greens fees. The money I received from the part-time caddy job helped us to get additional things to wear and pay some bills.

Caddying made me aware of the exciting game of golf. For a while I learned to play and did shoot in the lower numbers. Much to my sorrow, I had to quit because my disabilities became worse when I played; but I loved the game.

There was a time when we had no funds for anything but necessities. Today we laugh when we recall a frantic search in the pockets of all of our clothes, including Dottie's pocketbooks, to find enough money to buy two milk shakes at a local drive-in.

Once we had a hurried trip to Roanoke because of sickness in my family and after searching through all of our pockets, we finally found a small amount of money, which we used to buy gasoline. Many times I would almost coast to a service station just to save a few pennies. Dottie would say that I was going to run out of gas and would have to walk but I always made it to the gasoline pump.

I encountered a frightening experience one weekend while driving back to Williamsburg from Roanoke, prior to Dottie joining me. An eighteen-wheeler gasoline truck jack-knifed into the side of my car. Neither my passenger, Jimmy Johnson, nor I was hurt but this accident caused me to feel like the world was caving in on me. It took about three months to repair the car and pay the bill. During that time I was recognized around the campus as the guy who had plastic covering his car doors.

My memorable lawyer named Carneal, took money from the insurance settlement check prior to advising me of his fees. Saying, "Where I went to school they taught me to collect mine first," he demonstrated his lack of honesty, as I believe his price was unfair. He took his time, charged for every minute, every letter he wrote and each phone call he made, which conflicted with his original statements to me.

I later found out the irony of the situation – the service manager at the dealership was the lawyer's personal friend and neither would assist me unless I followed their advice. Needless to say, Colony Motors is not in business anymore. Maybe this type of activity caused its demise.

Another driving experience happened one day while I was driving Dottie down from the College Corner toward the Palace. A visitor began sounding his horn behind me. I did not know what was going on and tried to give him plenty of room to pass. At this time, the street had not been closed off to automobile traffic as it is now and cars were driving slowly to avoid hitting pedestrians.

The visitor continued to sound his horn and after about one block, I stopped my car and got out, lifted the hood and looked around as if something was wrong. The man was as mad as he could be, while his wife sat in the car laughing as hard and as loud as she could. After about sixty seconds, I lowered the hood and returned to my car without saying a word. All the while the other driver kept sounding his horn; then we both drove away without any fanfare.

In college, I majored in economics along with personnel management and psychology. When I began school, I found it difficult to study to put it mildly. However my visits to the library gave me a great incentive to read more and more. I became interested in words and their meanings.

Whenever I read, the words seemed to pop up into pictures formulated in my mind, which would coordinate with what the author was describing creating an impression on my thinking. The English language and the words comprising it impress me to this day. I cannot fathom how any American can take for granted such a beautiful language and not just love the flow of its words when used correctly.

Everyone studying at William and Mary was required to file reports of books he had read. Just a few of the topics required by the economics department included the book, *Money and Banking* along with statistics and a report on the *Wealth of Nations* written by Adam Smith in 1779. I found these topics fun and enlightening as well as challenging.

Because my themes and other writing assignments were important to me, I spent many hours in college researching material just to understand what the author was trying to impart. Looking back, I cherished the classes I attended. I don't recall being absent a single day.

Most of my professors were capable and informative in their presentations. They knew the topics under discussion and invented some assignments to force us to get outside our experiences to learn how the world was working.

But there was one professor who believed he knew everything and managed to say one thing and do another. Disgusted by his double talk, I failed his course – the only one I ever failed. His class was not extremely important to me at that time but now as I look back, I feel that my failure was not excusable. After all, it was only one course, and I should have been able to overcome this teacher's shortcoming.

I must recognize and show my appreciation with the utmost love to Dottie, who did the final typing of my themes and papers including typing my senior thesis even though I did the research in the library. My grades were based on the contents of the topic I chose, but her typing was impressive, neat and correct. This resulted in my obtaining higher grades – sometimes an A – because of her typing and corrections of my English or punctuation.

The final papers showed her expertise in education and language as an honor student in Business College in Roanoke. I probably would have been hard-pressed to find the same excellence she provided with her most impressive assistance in typing my written reports

I shall always remember the philosophy classes and the many discussions we had regarding life as presented by Plato, especially the attempt to understand the meaning of the soul. Additionally, the discussions in economics regarding finance, money and banking thrilled me.

I had an interest in botany and learned a lot from one of the professors, who gave me cuttings he had gotten from a hedge at a palace in England. When I moved to Norfolk I brought them with me and planted them. Believe it or not they are still growing and thriving, although their growth is very slow.

In June 1954, I graduated from William and Mary. I missed the classes and the fine professors who presented their lessons. To me the end of classes and especially my graduation came too soon.

But life must continue and each of us must learn other things as we travel through it.

To sum up my years at William and Mary in just a few words, I must say it was the most pleasurable time I have ever had. Sure, at times I felt in somewhat of a panic with all there was to learn and read while keeping my finances under control and making sure that I did not lose sight of my main objectives. But the subject material and the professors were as thrilling to me in the beginning as they were at the end of my classes.

Over the years I have made many visits back to the school, especially to the Economics Department and have made monetary contributions to encourage the average student to study harder, learn more about the great country we live in today and appreciate this fine school.

Steady Employment

In a business law class near the end of my last semester prior to graduating, I approached one of the professors, a retired Naval Officer and a reservist, to inquire if he knew where I might apply for a job. He suggested that I write to the District Intelligence Office (DIO) at the Naval Base in Norfolk, Virginia outlining my qualifications and indicating that I desired employment with the Navy as an investigator. I wrote a letter to the Navy captain in charge of the DIO and within a few days, received a reply scheduling an appointment for a job interview a few weeks after my graduation.

During the interview, which I anticipated with some anxious moments, I was questioned about my family life and military career during the war as well as my work aspirations. At the conclusion of the interview, I was informed that I must undergo a background investigation to determine my eligibility for employment. The process would take about thirty days before I would be notified.

The Cold War had begun in 1945 due to tension between the US and the former Soviet Union and its allies. Because of this, intelligence agencies recruited people to do investigative work.

While waiting to hear from the Navy, I secured a job with a contractor at Fort Eustis as a laborer and reported to work each day for about three weeks until my back gave out completely and I told the foreman I had to quit. He agreed with my decision, thanked me for being a steady worker, even for such a short time and wished me lots of luck for my future.

I received a special delivery letter informing me that I was to report to the DIO for immediate employment. This letter was written in an urgent tone with the expectation that I would arrive in a few days without taking into consideration that I had to move all my belongings, including some pieces of furniture. Also Dottie had to give notice to her employer before we moved to Norfolk.

I called the captain, explaining that I could not move my household to Norfolk without a place to live and that this would take several weeks to get everything in order, including paying my rent and getting utilities discontinued. Nevertheless, I informed him that my wife and I would come to Norfolk to seek living quarters within the next few days.

After making the necessary arrangements, we traveled to Norfolk where we made a deposit on an apartment we considered suitable for our needs near Gate Four of the U.S. Naval Air Station. While we were there, I went to the Captain's office and briefed him of my intentions and what we had accomplished.

He agreed to postpone my starting date for one week, saying that he was attempting to fill vacancies as rapidly as possible. We made the transition in the prescribed time and I began my new job after being sworn in as a federal agent for the District Intelligence Office, Fifth Naval District – a lower echelon of the Office of Naval Intelligence located in Washington, D.C.

I received briefings on my job description from the supervising agent but my main instructions, including the methods and laws under which I was to operate, were described in booklets from the Secretary of the Navy and Chief of Naval Operations and served as guides to be followed on certain investigations. I spent at least three days reading these books and pamphlets, some sections of which had to be explained by the supervisor.

Upon completion of the reading period, I accompanied another agent who would supervise me with on-the-job training – the only way to learn how to conduct an investigation. Over a period of months, I accompanied different agents, who gave additional indoctrination limited to the investigations we were conducting.

My expertise over months of inquiries and training began to center around criminal investigations within the Navy Department. However, a majority of the investigations at that time were for security clearances, which comprised most of the work at the office.

One incident I recall almost two years after I had been hired remains vivid in my mind because I thought this investigation was very odd. A prospective employee applying for a position as an investigator did not meet the educational requirements, but the commanding officer considered him a strong applicant.

However some of the applicant's neighbors did not speak highly of his wife who was a dancer. To my knowledge, there was never any illegal activity or question of the couple's loyalty but the captain wanted to personally interview the neighbors who made questionable comments regarding the wife's associates. He was concerned because none of the informants was willing to place their comments on paper and be sworn by affidavit.

As a result, I accompanied the captain to the neighbors' homes where he conducted interviews with me as a witness. Only then was he satisfied with the investigation and hired the person as an agent.

All new employees with no exceptions were required to undergo a full background investigation, not only of themselves but of their families as well, to ensure they had the proper morals and patriotic attitude. It was a prerequisite at that time for both military and civilian personnel who handled or controlled classified documents to receive a security clearance.

Eventually following my initial training, I received permanent credentials with DIO and became an accomplished street agent with investigations assigned to me. I furnished a written report of the details of each investigation and also dispatched leads that helped other agents throughout the world to conclude their investigations with details I provided from my local inquiries. I traveled throughout the Fifth Naval District in a Naval automobile.

The next two years Dottie and I continued living in the apartment near the Naval Air station. My work required me to travel extensively, not only in Norfolk or to Virginia Beach and Richmond but also entirely out of the area for days and sometimes weeks following leads sent to us.

Dottie and I finally decided to buy a house. We went hunting in many parts of Norfolk before we decided on a house in Meadowbrook Forest.

This three-bedroom ranch home pleased us in every way. The builder appeared to be reliable and honest. We moved in elated that we finally had a home to call our own for the first time since we were married.

This splendid house was desirable, not only for its location but also its solid construction. We were happy with it, with our neighbors and with the area. Unfortunately after two years, I received orders to transfer to Cherry Point, North Carolina to replace another person who had resigned.

The orders I received included doing background as well as other investigations on Navy and Marine personnel in an area that included Cherry Point and Camp Lejeune. I set up an office furnished by the Marine Corps at Camp Lejeune.

On many occasions, I had to travel to the Outer Banks of North Carolina by helicopter flown by Marine pilots from Cherry Point. I specifically remember one such flight when the pilot flew low enough to scare the wild horses. He announced over the radio that he was going in to land at the strip on Buxton, near the lighthouse. Almost immediately the aircraft pulled up abruptly and almost threw me out of my seat. When we landed he explained that he did not see a wire cable crossing the airspace until it was in front of him. At any rate although we did have a scare, we did not have an accident and everything was satisfactory.

Many times I traveled by automobile to Buxton, requiring driving over a hundred miles because the road went up to Elizabeth City, North Carolina then down the Outer Banks. This was almost an entire day of traveling, which became tiresome and expensive. I could submit a travel voucher for my time and expenses but I never did.

We had a difficult time locating suitable living quarters at Cherry Point. Housing was at a premium because the area was small with little ongoing construction. We finally were assigned to the Wherry Housing project, the only residential area available, unless we wanted to live in New Bern, North Carolina and travel about 50 miles to Cherry Point.

Dottie and I were not pleased with this type of housing but there were no other acceptable units. We were forced to live in an area with persons whom I subsequently had to investigate.

The house was dry but not the most comfortable place for us or for our furniture. In fact, Dottie was unhappy with the conditions from the beginning until we moved back to Norfolk three years later. The area consisted mostly of transient persons, which made it more difficult to cultivate friendships with neighbors. We were not accustomed to beer parties or large gatherings where profane language as opposed to proper English was the rule.

My area of responsibility encompassed Eastern North Carolina, including Camp Lejeune Marine base near Jacksonville. Most of my inquiries involved security investigations, eventually coming to revolve around criminal and subversive activities. Initially, some of the base investigators needed to see evidence that I was not a new kid on the block but eventually they accepted me as a qualified criminal investigator.

Toward the end of the 1950s, I was transferred back to the Norfolk Office. In the meantime because of the number of cases pending, the Norfolk Office decided to increase the number of agents to two at Cherry Point and five at Camp Lejeune. The supervisor decided that one person could not keep up with the workload. This was accomplished following my departure.

Of course I felt disappointed because of the long and arduous hours I spent working the entire area with no assistance or stenographic help of any kind. Following my investigations, I was required to type my reports and mail them to Norfolk where they were filed as a permanent record.

As part of the new procedures, secretaries were hired at both Camp Lejeune and Cherry Point, which made me feel used because of the long hours I worked attempting to complete many investigations without any secretarial assistance.

After deep consideration and many hours of discussions with Dottie, I finally requested a transfer overseas. But this request was denied with no explanation. I was moved back to Norfolk as a street agent.

Prior to moving back to Norfolk, we located the same contractor who built our original house on Meadowbrook Boulevard and entered into a contract with him to build our present home. Understanding that we would not be present during this construction, he gave us a sample drawing and began his construction while we were out of the area. There were some minor things we discovered wrong but overall he did a great job and we were pleased to recommend him to others who were considering building homes for themselves.

During the later part of the 1960s in an attempt to curtail the illegal use of drugs, commanders requested our office to furnish information to their personnel. Because I had investigated military personnel who abused drugs, it became my duty to lecture to the military organizations in the area about the horrors of drugs.

To prepare for the lectures, I studied various drugs and their adverse effects on the human body. I obtained samples of the drugs from a locked container where they were stored after they had been used as evidence. I gave thousands of lectures on ships and at the Naval Stations.

It required at least three hours to prepare one lecture using slides to show as much detail as possible. I spoke about the production of the substance and how it affected the human body, then answered questions afterwards. I have no knowledge if any of the military or civilian personnel decided not to use drugs as a result.

Most of the military personnel who used drugs chose marijuana. However some personnel used hard drugs when they went off base on leave. Occasionally they were hooked on cocaine, morphine or heroin, which is where I came in to investigate.

These investigations took place at almost every military installation in the area. Some were conducted with local police, state investigators, Drug Enforcement Agency (DEA), Customs, Secret Service and in later years, FBI agents.

When these agencies were in charge of an investigation, they appreciated our assistance in getting them to difficult places to interview suspects. I consider those agents friends. Once in a while when we see each other we talk about those days of our investigatory prowess.

One time, Custom agents visited our office wanting me to accompany them to a Navy ship arriving that morning. They had an informant who told them there was illegal whiskey aboard ship. These other agencies were happy to work with us and appreciated the way we could gain entrance to any space on the ships.

We apprised the commanding officer of our suspicions furnishing him most of the information and assured him a full report would be forwarded to him upon completion of the investigation. He allowed us to search the ship.

We located many cases of whiskey aboard the ship. Customs seized this illegal merchandise as evidence and arrested the military personnel for non-taxed alcohol. These personnel spent at least one night in federal custody then later appeared in federal court to be sentenced by the judge. They did not cause us any more difficulties.

One very sensitive case I began at Camp Lejeune had far-reaching aspects. It was a long, drawn-out investigation involving loyalty that most investigators will not forget.

I traveled extensively for twenty-two years, conducting most of the above types of investigations in our jurisdiction, the Fifth Naval District, which included Maryland, Delaware, Kentucky, West Virginia, Virginia and parts of North Carolina and Washington, D. C. The other districts worked the same way with leads sent back and forth among them to be covered and resolved.

There may be two or three investigations of murder or treason still pending where there is no statute of limitations. Some of the cases that were not resolved were murders of infants. I will never understand what an eight to nine-month old baby could do to defend himself against an angry father as in one case I investigated. The man subsequently convinced a psychiatrist that he had no knowledge of what he was doing when striking the baby's head and body against the crib and wall of the room.

Additionally, I cannot understand what possible results a person expected who destroyed a ship's engine with sand. The wrongdoer's motive was simple. He did not want to leave his family, girlfriend or other persons close to him.

But this behavior destroyed the engine and other working parts connected to it. In addition to the loss of time, the government had to spend a tremendous sum of taxpayers' money to replace the engine. Most importantly if there had been a national emergency, the warship could not have been used. During the Cold War, these sorts of actions affected many people.

In my investigations I have discovered that the culprits usually are young persons with little maturity who cannot fathom the expense to the taxpayer of such a large overhaul of a huge piece of machinery. Most of these crimes were committed in anger toward superiors and toward the Navy, which these people volunteered to join then later became disillusioned because something did not go their way.

At a later date, I met a sailor who was being tried for a crime I knew he did not commit. He was charged with sabotage of a ship's motors and engines. I had previously investigated this crime and determined another person had committed it. I immediately sought the sailor's lawyer, informed him of the circumstances of my investigation and revealed to him the real culprit.

I testified to convince the jury of my certainty that the man did not commit the crime. Subsequently the charges were dismissed. Another sailor, who was permitted to leave the service over my objections, had been the perpetrator.

Another case among many involved a cruel and gruesome murder. The murderer, a friend of the victim, if you care to call him so, stabbed the victim many times with a pair of scissors. Then he threw the weapon about fifty feet into a field with high bushes.

The body was found in a drainage ditch on a Friday evening just before securing time. It took many hours that night getting nosy military men away from the area so it could be preserved for evidence and additional daylight inspections.

In this particular case, although the officer in charge had been trained to preserve the crime scene for our investigation, he did everything wrong. His actions hampered my investigation so badly that eventually I threatened him with jail time just to get him to back away from the scene. The weapon was found and the blood matched the victim's. But the officer in charge compromised the evidence, which resulted in the suspect being released from the military without prosecution.

Once when President John F. Kennedy came to Norfolk for a visit, I worked in the detail with a Secret Service agent and an FBI agent to protect the President. When Kennedy departed the Norfolk Naval Air Station, I felt honored to have the duty of walking behind him up the ladder of the aircraft to protect his back with my body. The Secret Service always provided this protection for the President of the United States.

The day President Kennedy was killed in Dallas, Texas, I was on Church Street in Norfolk searching for a person who had sought shelter in a run-down building. In the poorly lighted entrance with a rickety stairway about to crumble and fall, a person walked toward me whom I could not identify in the darkened hallway.

I prepared to shoot the individual if he attacked or threatened to harm me but after the man spoke to me, I knew he was not the person I sought. After we talked for a few minutes, he told me where I could find the person I was after. He said this person was irresponsible and hardly anyone, even members of his own family, cared for him. He was described as a drug dealer who took advantage of everyone.

In fact his actions were such that this man told me not to turn my back on the people out in the street to whom I had spoken in my search. He said they would try to hurt me or kill me if they had the opportunity. Even to this day, I have not forgotten this information and I attempt to protect my back when I get into a tight spot.

These types of incidents, as well as shootings, homosexual conduct and suicides, became the norm for me to investigate and subsequently testify about in a court of law. Many incidents happened to me in the years of my investigatory activities and my miles of travels throughout the states as I attempted to determine the real evidence as opposed to the lies and misleading information.

My frustration would mount as a result of many people trying to cover up the identity of a suspect they erroneously believed was not guilty of anything. Eventually after serious inquiries with many informants, I would conclude the investigation and after an interrogation of the suspect and the presentation of testimony in court, the culprit would be convicted.

One of the most important aspects of the job, second only to the collection and preservation of evidence, was report writing. All agents had to learn this and each of the reports had to be written in such a manner that each interview became a small story. Then the entire investigation had to be written in detail and forwarded for permanent storage at the Office of Naval Intelligence in Washington, D.C. because as a general rule, the criminal cases were most likely to go to court and be heard by a jury.

In my capacity as a civilian contract employee working for the Department of the Navy, though my responsibilities cannot be enumerated in more detail, I was classified as a criminal investigator. My work involved following leads forwarded to us from other locations, including overseas, as well as initiating investigations within our local commands.

The investigations assigned to me included assault, arson, child abuse, fraud, burglary, and homicide. They included violations of Navy, Federal and Commonwealth of Virginia law as well as U.S. security breaches involving classified material.

At no time did I ever discuss the vast information in the files of the Naval Intelligence Service (NIS) in Washington relating to sabotage or questionable characters who might be security risks either from the United States or from other countries. I worked some of these cases in conjunction with the FBI, Secret Service, Customs and other recognized investigatory agencies. Perhaps my experience as a child in our unsolved house fire fueled my interest in doing this investigative work.

PART 4 RETIREMENT AND CONTINUING EFFORTS FOR JUSTICE

A Surprise Retirement

A few years before I retired in 1975, as I got ready to report for work, I passed out in the shower. Dottie awoke after hearing me moaning while the water was running. I remained in this condition until the rescue squad arrived at my home. After they examined me, they transported me to the hospital.

There our family physician called in a neurosurgeon who ordered x-rays. He determined that I had foreign matter just inside the right side of my skull and suggested an operation that same afternoon to remove the material. He believed that I acquired this substance from shrapnel that came from the shelling at Bastone the time I regained consciousness frozen to the water in the ditch.

I returned to work in about three weeks, continuing my regular investigatory duties assigned by my superiors. A few years later, this same neurosurgeon was assaulted. After the assault, he retired from the medical field, no longer able to perform any surgery, write consultations or discuss medical conditions. I have no idea where he is located. Nor do I know where the records of my operation were filed.

The hospital disclaimed any knowledge of the operation or the doctor. I wanted to locate these records to make them a permanent part of my VA medical history because I thought they would substantiate that my continuing migraine headaches were related to my military service.

Approximately one month following this surgery while I was again conducting investigations, I was assigned to assist the North Carolina Bureau of Investigations regarding the identity of a female body discovered in the Chowan River in Gates County, North Carolina. Based on the way her hands and feet were tied, we knew the perpetrator had to be a person who had knowledge of knots and how to tie a person so she could not get loose.

We began an intensive investigation, interviewing many military personnel. Using photographs of her dead body, we were able to identify her by name. Once we had her name, we kept asking questions and five days later, we had an address near the Little Creek Amphibious Base. We could not locate anyone in the neighborhood who could identify the dead woman but we located the house and forced open the door.

There was nothing in the building to indicate she was killed in that house. We did discover a photograph of her that we took with us as a means of identification. We finally learned that a Seal Team member was seen leaving the Chief's Club with her at closing time the night she was found in the Chowan River. It appeared this woman was familiar with many people who frequented this club.

We picked up a suspect for questioning but after interrogating him for many hours we learned very little about his habits or where he was the night of the murder. However we knew that he had been in Vietnam as a Seal Team member.

We had no solid evidence to link him to the murder. However according to the medical examiner, a farmer remembered seeing a car similar to his being driven toward the river in the early-morning hours on the date the woman was allegedly murdered. Unfortunately, the farmer did not recognize the driver nor did he obtain a license plate number.

As far as I know, this murder case is pending with no reasonable way of closing it. But I still believe our suspect was the person who killed this woman in North Carolina. We could never understand a motive because he had apparently spent the evening with her without any difficulty.

My supervisor withdrew me from the investigation because he believed that we in the Navy had investigated it sufficiently, using the proper methods and any culprit arrested would be tried in North Carolina courts. The North Carolina investigators congratulated me for the assistance I'd give them. Their supervisor said he hoped I would be living if he was ever found dead and no other person was around to help locate the murderer.

Almost immediately after the North Carolina investigation, according to military regulations, the time arrived for my yearly physical examination. I reported to the physician, a Navy surgeon who said he had to write up his findings about me in an official medical report. His examination was similar to ones I had gotten earlier although he was interested in my lower back and knees.

After we discussed my physical health and I answered his questions, he told me in no uncertain terms that I had to retire from my job or become an invalid as a result of my disabilities. He put that in his report as well as the operation on my head to remove the particles found by the former surgeon a few months earlier.

I delivered his report to my supervisor that same day. When the supervisor read the report, he became quite upset stating that I had not informed him of my physical condition earlier. This was untrue because my health record was available for him to review.

In any event, he demanded my weapon, credentials and badge immediately before I departed for my home – a complete surprise to me. The supervisor and the DIO subsequently decided that I must undergo another examination by a different physician. The inference was that I had not been truthful with the doctor at the examination.

I was told to report the following morning and clean out my desk. Accordingly, the following morning I gathered all papers, evidence and any government property in my possession and turned these over to another agent in the presence of the supervisor. This allowed the other agent to continue any investigations I had begun.

Prior to my leaving, the supervisor attempted to talk me into reporting for work each morning for the purpose of conducting interrogations and interviews to establish the identity of any culprit who had committed a crime. He assured me that I would not be boarding ships or going out of the office. This way I could remain on the payroll for a few more months and also be of benefit to the department.

This proposal sounded fine but I refused based on the orders of the surgeon who found me unfit for this type of work. Additionally, I based my decision on the past performances of the supervisors. It is my belief, which I have no way of supporting, that they made statements, changed their minds, then later denied changing their minds stating I had misunderstood their statements.

Within three or four weeks after I departed the office, I was instructed to report to another physician for a second opinion on my physical condition. The letter warned me that if I had misrepresented myself to the first physician, I could be in violation of the U.S. Code and could be prosecuted in federal court.

At no time did I ever attempt to hide my service-connected disability from any superior. In fact, I made a point of advising most of the special agents that I was rated 10% by the VA for a service-connected disability received as a result of my military service.

The second physician, located at NAS Oceana medical department, had known me for many years through the investigations I conducted. He was surprised to see me and expressed his dismay toward the supervisors who had sent me to him.

After he completed his examination, he told me he would write a letter setting a fire under the supervisor who did not believe the first physician. Within a few weeks following this second examination, I received a letter from the DIO and from the Personnel Management saying I would be retired in September 1975.

Needless to say, I was relieved that the affair was settled. Because of the back and knee pain, I was glad to get on with my retirement and the rest of my life. I did not miss required training in jujitsu or self-defense. All I wanted was to get a rest. Above all, I hoped to retrain myself for something I could accomplish without pain.

It was my intention when I retired to initiate a business of my own but as a result of my disabilities, I changed course and decided to learn clock repairing, which until then I considered a hobby. As a result of this interest, I met a man who agreed to teach me what he knew if I promised to go to school at the American Watch Makers Institute (AWI) where I would learn more about clock repairs. I agreed with his suggestion and studied with him every day for a year.

Then I went to AWI School in Cincinnati, Ohio. It was expensive and I was required to furnish my own tools as well as an old clock movement to disassemble, bush the pivot holes and then reassemble for inspection by the instructors.

As my former teacher predicted, I learned many more things at the school than anywhere else I might have gone for learning. We were even taught how to form mainsprings to fit each particular clock. In summation, the class and the instructors were fascinating, informative and gave me great insight into clock repair.

In horology or making timepieces, one must continue to learn and apply his skills. Even though a machine stamps out the wheels or gears, each clock movement is a little different, though the operations may be the same. The turning of the pivots is also challenging.

To repair the clock, it is necessary to understand the complete function as outlined by the clock maker. The answers may not be available from books on the topics written by some of the older clock makers. Because one can never get into the mind of a person deceased for many years who has made a time piece a certain way, the only way to find the answer is to try to reason why he made the clock and its movement as he did.

Clocks are similar to automobiles. They have to run just one way and if that system changes, a good machine will not function. This is why a person must study the way it was constructed.

I have never regretted this experience or the cost because it was something I wanted to accomplish and I have found it very rewarding. I have pursued the art of clock repair and at the same time been active in Chapter 21 of the Disabled American Veterans. Although very different, each has presented many worthy challenges.

The Disabled American Veterans (DAV)

Eight years before I retired, I received a letter from the Disabled American Veterans (DAV) in Cincinnati, Ohio informing me that as a result of my service-connected disabilities, I was qualified to join that organization. I received an application and pamphlets explaining the organization's purpose.

The representative powers described in this pamphlet intrigued me. I decided to send in my application. Subsequently, I was assigned to Chapter 21 of the DAV in Norfolk.

Then in 1975 the night before my Navy physical, I received correspondence from the chapter advising me of its meeting place in a savings and loan building in Norfolk. I decided to attend a meeting just to see first-hand what was happening and how this might affect my future.

I felt out of place and ill at ease with the eight people who were there at the first meeting. In my opinion I did not belong there mostly because of my reaction to the presiding officer who talked about the general affairs of the community, his job and what he and his wife liked about certain foods. He failed to mention the medical care that disabled veterans should be receiving from the Veterans Administration physicians, one topic in the brochure from Cincinnati that interested me.

After listening for a few minutes, I asked some questions and was told that the members of the chapter could not speak for the veteran, since they would not know the veteran's disabilities. It was my responsibility to go to the VA and talk to the doctors about my disabilities.

I asked why the DAV did not have service people to intercede and speak for the members. Again, it was stated that it was the individual's responsibility and if that did not work he should contact the National Service Officer (NSO) at the Veteran's Administration's regional office in Roanoke. Finally, after many questions, I learned that Richard Frazee was the contact person in Roanoke.

I complained that the NSO did not visit hospitals to get information from disabled veterans to submit to the adjudication board on their behalf. And why was information regarding the lack of medical care not submitted to the director of the hospitals? It was my belief and continues to be that VA medical care is lacking in substance and fails to follow an in-depth investigation into veterans' injuries in order to alleviate their pain.

I voiced my opinion rather sharply and supported it with the information I had read in the brochures. The chairperson and commander bluntly disagreed with my comments and attempted to belittle me. I learned later that another member, the treasurer who was a World War I veteran, wholeheartedly agreed with me, as did two other members.

As a result of my questions and the extremely harsh words from the commander including personal insults, I almost said, "Goodbye, good luck and I wish you well," to the Disabled American Veterans. I seriously considered joining another veterans' organization that might assist the disabled veteran. But I am not a quitter nor am I person to accept unsubstantiated off-the-cuff remarks such as those made by the commander. Therefore I decided to remain and see what would happen.

At that time about sixty members belonged to Chapter 21. However only about five or six persons attended meetings. The other members were housebound with no way to communicate with the officers of the chapter or members who could help them. The chapter members' records did not exist and to my dismay, not one person in the room could identify an additional person who was eligible to join the organization or work for the members.

After several meetings, I initiated a verbal resolution to have the chapter members contacted prior to the meetings in an effort to increase involvement within the chapter. Additionally, I initiated a resolution to allow chapter members to donate ten dollars at each meeting toward a building fund. This would eliminate the necessity of begging businesses to allow us to use their buildings for a meeting place. We would have a permanent place to store our flags or other accouterments that would be used during the meeting. The motion for a voluntarily donation was approved by the members and the meeting was adjourned.

At the next monthly meeting, however, as the minutes were read, I realized that I was misquoted on the motion. The recording person stated that I had mandated that all members be assessed regardless of their financial condition rather than voluntarily donating this money at every meeting. I strongly repeated the motion. It appeared that everything was understood. Then I made the first donation to the treasurer.

At this meeting, it was time for the chapter to nominate officers to be elected at the next meeting in June. Someone nominated me for the position of commander. I declined saying it would take some additional time for me to understand the organization's infrastructure. If I worked hard and learned the rules under which we operated, I might reconsider.

During the ensuing year, many discussions about fund-raising continued. A few members stated that I was a troublemaker. The auxiliary unit also took issue with motions I had made for the benefit of the veterans.

Each chapter member had to participate in the Forget-Me-Not drives to collect funds. In these drives DAV members offered flowers to those who contributed to our cause. At that time I was still working and even though I said my hours would vary, I was still assigned to a station.

Immediately following my normal working hours, I reported to the collection station at an Alcoholic Beverage Store (ABC), where I worked until the store closed. Two or three members handled the collections at most collection sites. We were required to take all funds collected to the commander's house even though he did not collect any donations, stating he was tired from working all day. He delegated this activity to the other members and officers.

There, after we counted the money, the commander called the police department to get an escort to the bank where the funds were deposited in an after-hours section. Sometime later, I made a motion that a day in the following week would be set aside to count the money so that those collecting could get some rest prior to counting the funds. The amount of money was small – less than two hundred dollars.

In order to get some semblance of continuity and to get the members to understand what I was trying to accomplish, I repeatedly stated the rules under which we operated, including the expenditure of Forget-Me-Not funds. This was based on my limited knowledge of the bylaws that I had access to at that time. But the members of the chapter and auxiliary ignored the bylaws published by the national organization. As I learned from conversations with the members, motions from the floor meant nothing to the chair.

During meetings, the commander's wife would invariably and obtrusively open the door to the next room where the auxiliary met and yell out, "We are opposed to the motions and will fight anyone who tries to force anything on us," and, "We will do what we want to at any time." Interestingly, my motions never involved the auxiliary unit but were confined to the chapter members.

I was appalled that the auxiliary controlled the chapter and dominated the members. The commander could not make any suggestions until his wife, the auxiliary commander, approved it. This woman made her comments without consideration for assisting the chapter or any disabled veteran, his widow or dependents, as was the auxiliary's explicit mandate under the bylaws.

At no time following such outbursts was I allowed to defend my position, since the commander did not recognize me. Everything that would be beneficial for the disabled veteran up to and including medical care at the VA was subject to the approval of the auxiliary. At a subsequent date I learned that the commander's wife knew nothing about the auxiliary's service responsibilities nor of the medical care furnished at the hospital.

Over a period of time I felt more and more disgusted and again was sorry I ever joined the Disabled American Veterans.

In 1973, election time for Chapter 21 came around. Following the election of officers, the chapter would sponsor a dinner for all members and their spouses. In accordance with the past procedures, funds from the chapter would be used to pay for the food unless "I wanted to make a personal contribution." I recall vividly that the auxiliary declined to make any contribution toward the dinner.

At this meeting, the membership elected me as commander and at the same time set the date for the installation of the elected officers for the regular meeting night in July.

Following my election as commander, I informed the membership that my time was taken by my employment and also that I had limited knowledge of the national organization or even the VA Department of Virginia. I asked the membership for their assistance in making the chapter the very best. At that time, my hours of work varied from eight to eighteen hours a day depending on the workload at my office.

The treasurer, with assistance from the commander and the auxiliary, planned the installation ceremony. I was informed that since I was new to the organization and not knowledgeable of the protocol, the outgoing commander would select the installing officer.

I did voice my reluctance toward someone being asked to install me whom I did not know. The members glossed over this and rather than cause arguments, I acquiesced, accepted this illegal maneuver and proceeded toward the unification of the chapter.

The treasurer selected the Naval Amphibious Base in Norfolk for the installation because he knew the personnel and the manager of the club there. The Club's past performance in furnishing good food to our members and guests had been completely satisfactory. Everything went according to plan. The affair was nice, the food was excellent and there were no complaints from either members or guests.

Since Chapter 21 had no meeting during the months of July and August, we could not accomplish anything until the next meeting in September unless I called a special meeting. However at a National Order of Trench Rats (NOTR) meeting a few weeks following the installation, I learned from one of the NOTR members that the immediate past commander and most of the former members including the entire auxiliary unit had transferred to Chapter 4 in Norfolk without telling anyone of their intentions.

Officers of both chapters had secretly planned this, probably months earlier. In the merger they had not only transferred members from Chapter 21 to Chapter 4 but they had transferred funds as well.

Naturally, I was disappointed and angry that they did not have the intestinal fortitude to discuss this openly but secretly attempted to scuttle everything we had planned for Chapter 21. I knew the outgoing officers and auxiliary carefully planned for me to fall flat on my face so they would have a scapegoat if things went wrong.

These people believed only in something for themselves rather than the future of Chapter 21 and the disabled veteran. I considered this action not in accordance with the precepts of the organization to assist the disabled veteran, his widow and orphans, as I had learned in the national bylaws. Again in my pursuit of justice, I decided to rectify this travesty of comical errors, which bordered on vengeance.

I coordinated the few members who decided to remain with Chapter 21. We obtained a bulk-mailing permit from the Postal Service and after a two-month delay while I waited for the national organization to mail me the names of eligible members, I personally set about writing two hundred individual letters each month to prospective members.

Two hundred was the number we needed to meet the minimum legal mailing requirements of the Postal Service for bulk-mailing procedures. Although it required time, it was worth the effort

We held Forget-Me-Not drives and planned several cookouts at the Veterans Administration Medical Center (VAMC) in Hampton where we also donated hospital items they needed. At that time we had no problem getting our members to participate.

I telephoned every known member of the chapter to talk with them about the projected goals for the chapter. Though my telephone calls were met with broad disenchantment by many, they were received gladly by a few who were interested in seeing the chapter prosper.

In addition, when we had Bingo on Sunday at the spinal-cord ward, I telephoned at least fifteen members on Saturday night urging them to attend. We astounded even ourselves by having fifteen or twenty members at every Bingo.

Our officers planned fund-raising dates very carefully, inspiring other members of the chapter to do something constructive to assist disabled and hospitalized veterans. As a result, we were able to increase our membership and plan for the future of the chapter and its members.

By the end of 1973 we had a host of projects planned and were growing stronger each month. Eventually we burst into full bloom as a viable chapter. The membership worked very hard to overcome many obstacles. They especially encouraged others to join us in helping disabled veterans.

Some of the older members told us that the city of Norfolk required us to go through Chapter 4 rather than our own Chapter 21 in order to get a permit prior to having a fund-raising function such as the Forget-Me-Not drive. We made a special trip to city hall to determine the correct procedure and establish personal contact with the proper official. There the Commissioner of the Revenue told us that we had been given wrong information, that our Chapter 21 permit was authorized and mailed the same day the city received our application.

Someone at Chapter 4 apparently held the permit until the day before our drive. Then they produced the authorization, telling us that the city delayed our request despite their attempts to get officials to hurry with the permit. This caused bitterness among our members, as our project was delayed. After this ridiculous incident, in order to overcome personal jealousies, we wrote letters to all of the chapters urging that we work together to produce a fine organization. We wanted everyone to feel proud to be associated with our organization.

I hoped that in the future these chapters would learn how to manage their business and recognize members of the DAV as friends rather than foes. My initiatives were realized slowly as it took almost ten years to achieve some semblance of cooperation, communication and coordination of activities.

As a result of Chapter 4's interference, we incorporated Chapter 21 to make sure that nothing like this would happen again. Things have not been a bed of roses, but Chapter 21 has emerged as one of the best chapters in the Department of Virginia. This was not because of me but the efforts of our members, who took part in building a better chapter and kept up the pace with phone calls trying to recruit more members.

Sponsoring other activities, offering programs and communicating with members brought most of our older members back into the chapter. Our drive to inform the members of Chapter 21 spilled over to other local chapters. They kept asking questions about our methods of operation and we explained that we were not attempting to do any harm to them. We were all disabled veterans trying to communicate and have a better cooperative understanding with all chapters.

We in Chapter 21 have never intended to overpower or disrespect any other local chapter. In fact the reverse is true. We attempted to inform all other chapter members of what we were doing. However we experienced very little success because someone always found fault with a member of Chapter 21 and especially with me as I later learned.

In 1974 Chapter 21 initiated a forum, Commanders and Adjutants, in an attempt to iron out misunderstandings and maintain a harmonious relationship among chapters. But the idea was trivialized and met with excuses because the desire of others was to get ahead of Chapter 21.

Organizational Changes

DAs time progressed and our membership grew, we decided that the best way to get our members to learn more about the organization was to change our election from June to March. That would allow the new commander and other elected officers to go to the statewide convention knowing they could speak for the entire chapter.

There was some controversy about this with some saying that we have always done this in July so why change and cause confusion? However, this argument did not prevail, the change in procedure was accomplished and we continued to proceed with changes to our bylaws and rules that have been satisfactory in every respect.

Prior to my becoming a member of the DAV, the Department of Virginia voted that each chapter would donate 10% of the highest fund-raising project to this department. At that time, the department had very little operating funds. We in Chapter 21 never defaulted on these donations and were always prompt in forwarding our funds. However, we learned later that other chapters were not as philanthropic with their funds.

After I joined the DAV and attended the conferences and conventions, I became knowledgeable of the organization's functions by participating as a member of committees. This afforded me an opportunity to have input toward the betterment of disabled veterans especially the ones who could not get around as well as I could at that time.

My appointment to the bylaws committee encouraged many of our chapter members to become active in other department programs by attending conventions and conferences. This was one way to help them with their claims and eventually their finances. We were not interested in obtaining monetary compensation for our members. We were mostly interested in members getting the proper medical information to finalize their claims with the VA.

To get medical information, we set up programs to have the National Service Officers (NSO) and others speak to us about obtaining written information from our doctors and also about the medical care we should receive from the VA. We initiated a program to fund the NSO when he visited. This program was a hit with all of our members, with many asking questions and receiving answers.

Finally, we changed the bylaws of the department to discontinue donations from the chapters. Many chapters struggled to make ends meet and comply with the bylaws while the department was becoming financially satiated.

The Department of Virginia needed a budget to pay the elected officers and other committee members' expenses and further the solidarity of the chapters. At the outset of this resolution, former officers opposed the funding, stating that in the past all officers paid their way from personal funds. They believed that any person within the department who wanted to get ahead in the organization should work hard thereby gaining recognition for a job well done.

This resolution caused bitterness and many foul words from those already in elected office who felt left out when the resolution was presented. Prior to the passage of this resolution, past department commanders opposed any person receiving funds regardless of his office. This caused newly elected officers and committee chairmen to be denied funds and forced a person who aspired to an office to pay his own way regardless of his financial status even though the business he conducted favored all disabled veterans.

Eventually, the popular persons were elected while other qualified persons were passed over. This is not to say that the Department of Virginia has less well-educated persons achieving higher office. What it says is that most persons who are not known have an unequal chance of becoming commander.

Additionally the Department of Virginia copied the national organization by preventing persons from speaking from the floor by turning off the microphone from the podium.

At a department convention a few years ago, I decided to test the department administration on a provision in the national bylaws which states that once a person is a member he will not have to pay any more dues or fees. Therefore I decided to attend the business session without paying the registration fee.

To my astonishment, the sergeant-at-arms informed me that the department adjutant required that I pay a five-dollar fee to register and receive a nametag to identify myself. I refused, asking the reason for this request. I was informed that the former national adjutant was believed to be in the hotel and might try to attend our meeting.

The former national adjutant had been accused of taking money from the organization to use for his personal gain. This accusation, like others based on personal opinion, contributed to my refusal to attend any more conventions or conferences. It is my opinion that the members of DAV should have the opportunity to attend any function, even if they have no legal right to vote. This has not been the case.

Additionally over my objections, the chairperson of the finance committee denied me the opportunity to sit in on a meeting where a member of Chapter 21 was discussing one of my resolutions. To my knowledge, the chairperson has never been corrected or admonished for this infraction. In fact, she was promoted.

I believe that if a person has his DAV card and appears at the doorway of an ongoing meeting, he should be allowed entrance. Let the card speak for the member but do not disqualify him on the premise that someone else might do harm to the group.

Thrift Store Operations

All chapters of the Disabled American Veterans in the Tidewater Area lacked funds to proceed with assistance programs especially those at the VA Hospital in Hampton. We discussed many ways to raise funds to help these veterans. We also considered ways to help the chapters by building or renting space to care for the veterans, their widows and their orphans, as mandated in our bylaws. Naturally these concepts brought many questions to the forefront.

In February 1972, Thomas Mizel (now deceased) invited each of the five chapters in the area to attend a meeting at Chapter 41 in Portsmouth. The purpose of this meeting was to discuss a thrift store operation that would provide funds to sponsor activities at the Hampton Veterans Administration Medical Center (VAMC).

Of the five chapters, one declined outright to participate because its members did not want to engage in "junk" dealing. Another expressed disinterest. The others, though having little knowledge of thrift stores, finally showed a willingness to oversee this operation. Tommy Mizel agreed to write letters to Mr. Robert O. Ellison and Mr. James DePew, whom he met at a Commanders and Adjutants meeting on thrift store management in Washington, D. C. A meeting was scheduled for the following month. We were about to experience the meaning of "red tape."

In the meantime, in accordance with the bylaws, we wrote a letter to the department commander asking permission to form a thrift store in Norfolk. Prior to our next meeting after writing two additional letters, we finally obtained the permission.

But the commander also requested that permission be obtained from the national organization. Additionally, we would be required to obtain a contract from Mr. Ellison, which would have to be submitted to the state and national organizations for review and approval.

We initiated a letter to the national organization to obtain a management agreement and contract with Mr. Ellison, requesting approval of our thrift store operation and apprising the office that the Department of Virginia gave its permission for us to enter into this contract. We included a summary report of our meeting, including our elected officers, Roy Mitchell (now deceased) from Chapter 6 as president, Thomas Mizel as treasurer and me as secretary. The approval was granted within sixty days.

When we obtained the approval to enter into a contract with Mr. Ellison, he visited Norfolk to search for a building to rent, which he found on Kempsville Road in Norfolk. To our dismay a restaurant business adjacent to the building served us with a notice of rejection because its owners considered the thrift store a junk store that would conflict with acceptable business practices.

In response to this rejection, Mr. Ellison secured an attorney who filed a petition in the Norfolk Court. The judge ruled that the thrift store was a business that we, as a recognized charity were qualified to operate at that location without any interference. After the judge's decision, we opened the store and from that time we have had no unfavorable comments that would place us in jeopardy.

The store manager was and continues to be Mike Hudson. He and his wife, Linda, worked many hours handling and sorting clothing for sale. Their efforts have been remarkable and we have received funds for our many projects. A few of our members have complained about Mike's salary but I always reply, "If he makes money, we make money. It's that simple."

The restaurant owners who complained about our locating there closed about two years later. Contrary to their fears, our business brought in more patrons to their restaurant, allowing it to prosper for the short time they were next door.

Eventually, we outgrew the space and needed to move. We decided to build our own store about a half mile away. This required securing a piece of property in Virginia Beach and hiring a contractor. That store remains profitable, continuing to furnish funds for the thirteen local chapters to this day.

Eventually after Roy Mitchell became ill and decided to bow out of the presidency, I was elected president. At that same time, two newly-formed chapters wanted to participate in the thrift store venture. At Chapter 2's opening ceremony in Newport

News, they requested recognition as well as funds from the thrift store.

As President, I welcomed them as members. However the other officers were not in favor of this. I said to the members of Chapter 2, "A disabled veteran is a disabled veteran, regardless of his location on the face of the earth."

At the opening ceremony there were members visiting from other chapters who had the same opinion as the other officers. They cursed me and threatened to have me expelled from the DAV because I made remarks of which they had not been previously informed. These people and members of the thrift store committee apparently did not know that I too had not been asked about other chapters joining our organization in order to share the future funds.

Later they, along with other members in the local chapters, wrote letters continuing to threaten me for giving their money to another chapter that did not do anything to help develop the thrift store. But to set the record straight except for the elected officers (of which I was one), none of the other chapters did anything to further the future of the thrift stores either.

As a result of these letters, I resigned the presidency of the thrift store at the next meeting and walked from the front desk. But I did not leave the meeting. I stayed there to make things more difficult for those who thought they excelled with superior knowledge regarding thrift store operations.

Thereafter, I channeled my thoughts and energy toward Chapter 21. We discussed the funds and much to my surprise, the members were not interested in dividing funds with additional chapters in the same area.

Finally I repeated the phrase that to me was paramount, "A disabled veteran is a disabled veteran, regardless of his location in the universe." But this comment was unacceptable to the others whose attitudes and words displayed greed from the outset. In the end we agreed that we would not allow additional chapters to get funds unless there was solicitation in the chapter's area or city.

Since we in Tidewater had our own thrift store, I suggested that other chapters in the Department of Virginia could profit from a similar operation. At our regular meeting, I offered to discuss the formation of another thrift store with the other chapters. After a short discussion, most members accepted the suggestions I offered.

At our next department convention, I submitted a resolution to the members asking them to endorse a thrift store for the Department of Virginia. This resolution was worded to exclude the chapters that already had a source of income from a thrift store. Most persons holding office within the department benefited from the idea, as did the individual chapters without a thrift store. The members could attend the conventions and conferences from their respective chapters out of thrift store profits without having to pay for the expenses from their individual funds.

Eventually it was accomplished but not in the way it was proposed at the beginning. The other members of the department opposed chapters having funds, thinking chapter members would not know what to do with this additional windfall if it were approved. I proposed to give 10% to the department and divide the remaining funds equally between the other chapters that had no thrift store or other source of income. But at the insistence of a few persons, the resolution was changed to suit certain individuals and chapters who might have only a personal need for the funds.

Before I resigned, I requested a review of the funds from the management company and a projection of the likely income each chapter would receive in the future, based on the recorded store income. The management company agreed with my thoughts and decisions.

In the course of these discussions we finally agreed that we needed a CPA to handle our accounting and for the past ten years we have had a good one. At the present time, we are seeking a small company to handle our administrative work, such as writing letters, sending out notices and other tasks we have been unable to accomplish.

My association with the management company has been on firm ground, with no negative evaluation of me. As events changed for the better and I developed a good association with the local store manager, an expert in problem solving, I decided to again become president of the thrift stores and was elected by the membership of the several chapters involved.

Prior to my acceptance of this post, I realized that the Virginia Beach store needed an addition to its building as well as a larger parking lot for customers. The membership also voted to build a store in Newport News. Over the objection of some members, we purchased the land for this and granted the building committee the authority to proceed to establish another management corporation.

This procedure required obtaining loans from the bank and submitting legal papers to the city courts and the banks. The officers approved these procedures, and the committee assigned to these tasks finally resolved everything to the advantage of all concerned.

Following extensive, expensive and laborious negotiations over a period of six or eight months, I finally requested that I be given the single authority to finalize the purchase of the property for our thrift store parking lot and get on with the renovation of our building. Without the presence of lawyers or accountants, I met over a cup of coffee with the landowner and we signed an agreement to allow the parking lot extension and the renovation of the Virginia Beach store. The extended parking lot has made a terrific impact on the funds coming into the thrift store and to the local chapters.

Trouble in the Organization

Around the same time as the Virginia Beach store expansion, a National Service Officer (NSO) allegedly made remarks at a convention regarding the department commander, the adjutant and the chief of staff who responded by writing a letter to the national commander condemning the NSO and his character. Even if the NSO had made the alleged remarks, the officers had no reason to write letters to the national organization condemning him for them.

This was character assassination, constituting improper, dictatorial and unwarranted conduct on the part of the department commander, his adjutant and his chief of staff. The national service officer had done nothing wrong except to speak openly at a convention.

As a result, I wrote to the department executive committee requesting that these three elected officers be recalled and others be elected to replace them. Following this request, I experienced similar harassment. I was accused of taking another disabled veteran's wife to these affairs for my own personal satisfaction.

The discussion about the recall went on for about three months. Except for two or three others who did not want to become involved by name, I was the only one involved in the resolution to remove these officers. However, many others were present at a meeting I called in Richmond to air the complaints and proceed with the campaign I had begun. The end result, to my dismay, came about when the NSO in Roanoke stated that the national adjutant wanted all material in my possession forwarded to him for review and final decision.

None of the persons involved was ever disciplined; but the commander, following his term of office, did not return to the meetings and the chief of staff was transferred to a national chapter after he made ungentlemanly comments including untruthful statements about another matter.

It must be noted that the commander of the department ordered all officers not to attend the meeting I called in Richmond or they would be tried and convicted for violation of his orders.

Because of this, my opinion of the elected officers in the DAV Department of Virginia declined even further.

Later, prior to the next convention, the department commander, who was still in office at that time, contacted the national organization stating that Chapter 21 refused to submit its financial records for an audit. This forced us to take our financial records to the convention for review by a former national commander who found no irregularities in them.

Following this audit, the representatives from Chapter 21 were allowed to be seated and could vote on any topic. About two years later, this former department commander approached me at a conference and wanted to shake my hand. He said I was correct in what I had said previously even though by that time I had forgotten most of the details.

Around this same time, an audit of the department indicated there were missing funds. After I was recognized by the chair to speak, I refused to yield the floor until I was heard completely. Eventually the treasurer was relieved of his duties because he had directed the missing funds to his personal use. There has never been a report to the membership on the amount missing or what happened when the board met and made a decision.

As a result of my actions I am still considered a troublemaker and mostly persona non-gratis within the DAV Department of Virginia but I could care less. I knew I was correct at that time and still believe so.

Ironically, about ten years ago the department membership was asked to reinstate this former treasurer as a member in good standing. He claimed to have been ill and not to know what possessed him to do such a dastardly act. I must admit that I was one of the members who spoke against him and the resolution to forgive his acts.

Most of us have seen soldiers die because of poor decision-making and reluctance on the part of those in charge to carry out direct instructions. This was no exception. In my opinion he deliberately and unwisely defrauded the DAV Department of Virginia by taking funds he was entrusted to protect.

At the present time, we have thirteen chapters in the local organization. We incorporated the stores in order to stall frivolous court-action suits. As was stated previously, seven chapters began to prosper and furnish benefits to their members. Then other new chapters earned their way into the group and all have made sufficient funds to carry on the service work enumerated in the bylaws of the DAV.

There have been others who tried to form splinter groups in an attempt to get funds from the thrift store but these fell by the wayside. In fact, the DAV Department of Virginia, using a subtle maneuver, attempted to take over the stores but was repulsed by a majority vote. However our national organization has dealt us a low blow by incorporating into the bylaws of the national organization a provision giving the state organizations the authority to eventually supervise the operation.

This is a travesty – an insult to those of us who have worked and struggled to mount a viable thrift store operation to assist the disabled veterans in the area. The only thing it shows is greed on the part of the department and national organizations.

The national organization and its hired civil lawyer objected to the stores by canceling all contracts after they had been operating for about five years, even though their executive committee previously approved them. As a result of their actions, we were forced to write letters to the national organization threatening a counter-suit.

As an afterthought, the department opened two or three stores of its own requiring management skills, which in my opinion, the department does not possess. These stores have since gone under without providing any funds to be divided among the outlying chapters.

Finally, the national organization sent a contract for us to sign that was not as protective as our original contract. It is understandable to a certain extent why the national organization wanted to protect the local chapters and afford them with the largest amount of funds available. However, the contract excluded many paragraphs found in the original contract that protected the local chapters as well as the DAV personnel.

During all of the discussions, we succeeded in getting management to open a thrift store in Hampton named the Outlet. This store produced excellent funds for all of us. However some of the members of the DAV decided that they were still not getting sufficient funds and talked other members into believing the same. As the months passed, these members convinced other members of the corporation to sell the Outlet to management, a bad decision in my opinion.

The manager hired to operate the Outlet was renting it from the owners on a square-foot basis and making a grand profit, not only for them but for us as well. Once management began discussing selling the store, the allure of profits clouded the eyes of many members. Problems arose when some of them began talking of becoming management themselves thinking they could make more money.

A few members got together quietly and formed a corporation, which they then presented to the membership at our next meeting. Some of the members did not understand what had happened and voted for the new corporation on the basis of friendship for those in this group rather than on an objective basis. At that time management offered to buy us out, which would allow us either to continue under them or to use another firm – the new corporation – to operate the store.

When some heard what it would cost the chapters to run the store, they decided the price was too high, even though the funds would be deducted in installments on a monthly or yearly basis. At the insistence of these few members, a majority of those present voted to sell the Outlet to management rather than purchase it.

This transaction worked badly and in order to stay on the peninsula with another store, we had to rent a building. This cost the DAV many thousands of additional dollars. In addition, we had to pay start-up costs to the new corporation. We rented two stores in the hope that there would be more income to help us survive on the peninsula.

To ensure this survival, we entered into extraordinary planning to build another store in Norfolk or Virginia Beach, a plan authorized by the members of the corporation at a regular meeting. A few of us began to emerge as take-charge leaders, rotating new personnel as the corporation officers, and we eventually concluded a contractual arrangement for buying large pieces of property in Newport News and in Virginia Beach. We were aware that paying a large mortgage would be difficult but we negotiated with the bank to pay a certain amount at the outset and then, when we accumulated sufficient funds, to pay more to lower the interest and the principal.

On one occasion we foolishly entered into a contract with a management firm after the sale of the Outlet in Hampton and eventually discovered they were charging us with administrative and other fees. When we met with them, they argued that we agreed to those fees, which was what the government did with all contractors. We disagreed, and the situation went to arbitration, as the contract stipulated.

The arbitration board agreed with us and we were paid over $200,000 from the management firm. They in turn filed for bankruptcy and went out of business.

Our stores' sales became remarkable, increasing each month and lasting for many years, even with the rent on the two stores in Hampton. Two years after securing the bank loans, we began paying each of the thirteen chapters a small amount of money – considerably more than each received at the outset of the contract in 1973. As more money became available, we increased the amount to each chapter. As I remember, the amount began at $2,500 every quarter and it continues to increase each quarter.

The Thrift Store Corporation has a single contract with management for the Virginia Beach store and a single contract with management on the peninsula. These contracts grant the corporation or chapters ten percent of the gross sales, with management getting the same. However if any funds are left over after management pays all bills, including salaries of employees, taxes and rent, the corporation for the DAV Thrift Store gets the remainder, to be divided equally with all thirteen chapters.

Most of these funds are still being used for service work for disabled veterans. Computers, copiers and fax machines cost money, and we assist the disabled veteran as set forth in the bylaws, using these machines for that purpose.

In our dealings with the national organization, it has become not only disheartening but also really insulting when we receive notification stating, "You have 30 days to respond to this request. Failure to do so will result in the removal of your Charter." This means the chapter cannot conduct any business until the requests have been met in every respect according to the national organization's demands.

In grade school and even in high school, threatening comments were the norm. But we are adults and have been shot at, kicked around and cursed by many people and groups. I find these threatening letters from the DAV national organization, where the anointed has spoken and demanded us to comply, unnecessary and demeaning to say the least.

However after writing letters of complaint to the national organization, including a summary from an attorney who threatened to enjoin the national organization in court for canceling the contracts, we finally have a thrift store with incoming funds that the chapters can use to benefit needy disabled veterans, their widows, and orphans in a dignified manner.

We have had a super time with the thrift stores giving the members, old or new, something to hang on to. When we sponsored parades for both Memorial Day and Veterans Day, we tried to include patients at the Hampton Veterans Administration Medical Center (VAMC) in the outings. We could not have had these assistance programs without funding.

This is not to imply we had no problems, nor does it mean we are wealthy. But the problems were resolved by working out solutions to the satisfaction of all disabled veterans in all of the chapters. At the present time we have one store in Hampton, one in Newport News and one in Williamsburg, along with the one that was moved to Virginia Beach from Norfolk about ten years ago.

Even with the adverse feelings and condemnations from the national organization and the Department of Virginia, we have prospered, accomplishing many fine projects to help not only the chapter but also the membership and deserving disabled veterans.

At the present time, I am the only person of the original group to be alive and I might add that I continue to exert constructive influence toward the thrift stores, which has not set well with a few members. I have admonished some of the younger persons who believe money grows on trees and all they have to do is ask for the funds without any work or forethought.

We have a good relationship with the original management of our Virginia Beach Store, which is continuing in business. However at the outset, it furnished only a very small amount of money to the local chapters. Initially this money appeared large since we had not been accustomed to getting funds to spend on our functions to assist disabled veterans. We felt prosperous with the small amount we received.

This type of funding did not go unnoticed by most of us in an elected position and we negotiated with management for additional funds. We were aware that our portion of the funds was estimated to be 4% of the gross received. We began a negotiated deal to get additional funds from management and were in the process of getting another contract.

In fact we had a verbal agreement that would eventually be in writing for us to get at least eight percent of the gross. However, the national organization cancelled all contracts, and we had to alter our procedures. Eventually the national organization demanded that the chapters receive 10% of the gross from the thrift stores' management. This agreement is in effect today.

My tenure with Chapter 21 has not been a bed of roses. Nor has it been extremely unpleasant. However as I've said before, there have been times I wished that I had never heard of the DAV based on the knowledge I have gained about the organization and the members at all levels.

The bylaws state that Robert's Rules must be the parliamentary authority. I agree with this. However, each chapter must write its own bylaws, taking care that they do not conflict with the department or national bylaws. But when an elected official inserts his or her own ideas, mandating that everyone abide by his procedures and ignoring the bylaws and rules, something is not right.

I have no objection to change when the changes are reasonable and sound; however changes on whims or merely the bright ideas of some of the elected officials are not always in the best interests of the disabled veteran.

The national organization has mandated that any member of the organization may be elected to any office. I appreciate this thinking; but how in the world can a brand new person off the street assume the office of commander of an organization when he knows nothing about the demographics or the logistics? Furthermore, the rules have been altered so that any member of the military, not only the disabled veteran, may become a member of the DAV. To me this is diluting the organization.

The pain of surgical operations and medical procedures on the human body will last as long as the patient lives and the disabled veteran will experience these discomforts more than others. Anyone in charge of an organization wants to look good in the eyes of his peers in his or other organizations. Setting goals for oneself to increase the organization's membership is one way to achieve this esteem.

However when the numbers are increased, the veteran who has been getting medical care will get fewer visits and fewer medical treatments from the limited number of VA doctors. And the number of qualified physicians has decreased.

Is this progress? Is this giving the veteran – especially the disabled veteran – better treatment? I think not. Additionally, most physicians at the VA fear being sued for prescribing drugs to relieve pain. The only rationale I can perceive for this is growth of the membership, causing a decided reduction in medical care.

When I first joined this organization, the pamphlets and brochures highlighted a caring DAV with an established, almost around-the-clock program of confronting the VA doctors when they did not furnish the proper care to the patient. These congenial and well-prepared encounters favored the veteran as much as possible.

And generally speaking, the national service officers who intercede with the VA on behalf of the disabled veteran, attempting to get medical service for those who are in need, have done well and are a credit to the DAV. To those whom I know personally, I must say that my hat is off to them for a great job helping the disabled veterans in filing their claims and representing them before the VA adjudicating boards.

The founders of the Disabled American Veterans, originally under a different name in 1921, had a wonderful idea whose underlying theme was to allow disabled veterans to operate their organization by democratic methods.

But today it generally does not work as was originally planned. The rules change from day to day and it appears that the national administration wants to build a million-man organization disregarding membership qualifications as to whether the person has been disabled, injured or wounded while in military service during time of war or conflict. The administration seems to be trying in every way to maintain its course regardless of the future outcome.

In my opinion, the bylaws are not followed. Ludicrous ideas are brought in and interpreted as long-standing policy by leaders who want to rule and govern rather than lead. This is completely ruining the great organization conceived by our founders.

There are disabled veterans who are not treated by the VA for their injuries and pains because of overbooking by improperly trained clerks who fill the physicians' offices daily with patients. These persons' complaints do not meet the criteria under which the DAV was formed.

Benefiting Disabled Veterans

Each of the thirteen DAV chapters now receives over eight thousand dollars per quarter to use as they wish. However, the national organization has mandated that the chapters spend about fifty percent of these funds toward service work to help the disabled veteran, his widow and orphans.

I can truthfully state that Chapter 21 does exactly this and has been doing it for many years. We furnished washing machines, dryers and other equipment to the Veterans Administration Center in Hampton and have furnished other things to local organizations that are helping disabled veterans.

We donated most of the funds – over $80,000 – for a new bus to carry patients to functions away from the hospital, soliciting this sum from other veterans' organizations and donating our personal hours to work on the project. Our members collected funds at places such as Reggie's pub at Waterside in downtown Norfolk, where we spent many nights collecting from patrons with the consent of the management.

We informed the patrons where the money would be spent and how we would continue to obtain funds until we reached our goal. To my knowledge neither our members nor our chapter has received any credit for this or other similar accomplishments.

Our chapter also bought and presented a van to the Hampton Veterans Administration Medical Center (VAMC). Unfortunately, it appears that this van is being used to transport working materials to various parts of the hospital grounds. We do not approve but have no control over the use of the van because we donated it to the Medical Center.

We also worked at many establishments to earn funds to purchase the van doing volunteer work without receiving VA volunteer credit to the chapter or to the individual. Our members have spent many hundreds of hours in performing these services to assist disabled veterans to receive proper medical treatment.

We also have transported disabled veteran's families to outlying cities for medical treatment. Our members drove the families in their own personal vehicles without pay.

Our estimate of what we've spent on these goals has been over 65% of what is allocated in the national organization bylaws and conceivably could be much more. Were I not involved in the thrift store operations, I would not be in a position to furnish the above information but I am happy to report that on a scale of one to ten, Chapter 21 is rated near the top.

In the beginning when I originally was elected commander of Chapter 21, I personally financed my trips to the department conferences and conventions knowing full well the chapter did not have any available funds for me. I did this to obtain information to report back to our members, thus benefiting our chapter.

Eventually, I began to take other members of the chapter along with me, including members of the new auxiliary who were willing to attend. Slowly, we increased our funds to pay the registration fees for our members to attend the conferences and conventions. Eventually we expanded the funds to cover meals and rooms and finally to include mileage. In this way the chapter membership learned about the Department of Virginia and the DAV organization, its rules and procedures.

Some chapter members demanded funds for personal use, which as commander, I declined to honor. Some of our former members began to question the travel activities and eventually things became rude, impossible and even at times crude. I decided to discontinue my philanthropic practice of paying my own expenses.

One member requested the chapter purchase him an automobile basing this on the limited compensation he received for his expenses. Many sarcastic comments came from other chapters in this regard.

Because DAV members condemned me erroneously on many charges, I decided at Dottie's insistence to demand the DAV pay my expenses. In Dottie's words, "The DAV members are using you and our funds," and she was entirely correct. She was not angry but she was opposed to my underwriting expenses on my own when the other members did not contribute their funds to the chapter to benefit disabled veterans.

We in Chapter 21 have been members that operate for the benefit of veterans, especially disabled veterans. Our membership has been active in most cases but as time goes on we have become physically less able to participate.

In 1998 as in previous years, our membership voted to purchase Thanksgiving baskets as well as gifts for families of disabled veterans and their children. We extended this effort to Christmas as well because we discovered there were families of disabled veterans who were in need of cheer as well as food.

We used the income obtained from the thrift stores to fund many of these projects. None of the members of our chapter were paid salaries nor did they receive funds from the thrift stores in exchange for their involvement. If there was a need to pay for any of the presents, food or clothing, we gladly used our funds for this purpose.

There are people within the organization who have demonstrated excellent attitudes, workmanship and above all, a desire to help those who are in need. I can truthfully state that members of Chapter 21 as a whole have been supportive and helpful in every way.

A New Building

As has been mentioned, we had about sixty inactive members and a bankroll of fifty dollars when this all began shortly after I joined the chapter. Since that time we have met in various places, including a church or two or in rooms other organizations rented to us for our meetings.

Over a period of years, we discussed having a chapter headquarters building as a permanent place to store our flags and other items. Carrying them from place to place for our meetings became a burden on one or two persons. In addition, they had to locate storage space and a vehicle to transport our supplies if we received a firm answer from any business that we could use its space.

Finally, we sent letters to the adjutants of each local chapter, setting a date and place for a meeting. Only two other chapters sent members, making the meeting unproductive. Even with a specific invitation, members were not willing to discuss ways to improve the relationship of the DAV members locally.

In our next attempt for cooperation we hosted a meeting of all local chapters with a dinner prior to the department convention to discuss policies and submit resolutions to help all disabled veterans and chapters. Unfortunately, this idea succeeded on only one occasion; but it provided a good sounding board for all persons who attended. I later learned that when some members heard that I had initiated the affair, they stayed away or would not comment pro or con.

At one of our regular meetings of Chapter 21 (held in an Elks Lodge for a $35-per-night fee) we discussed the topic of our own building. The discussion was loud with some voicing strong opinions. Two or three persons in the chapter were not in favor of a permanent building. They believed that all funds we had should be donated to the Hampton Veterans Administration Medical Center (VAMC) without any restrictions. Other members disagreed with this statement.

Those in attendance agreed to a special meeting to be held prior to the next regularly scheduled meeting to vote on the topic of a building for the chapter. Each member present knew that no other topic would be discussed at this special meeting because under Robert's Rules of Order, which we were following, all other discussions were barred.

This special meeting, which was announced by letter, began with the opening ceremony and a roll call ensuring that every member's vote would be counted. When the question of the headquarters building was brought to the floor, the votes were recorded by name.

The majority voted for a building named Headquarters for Chapter 21 Disabled American Veterans. At the conclusion of this special meeting, a committee began to search for a building or land to build on. As I recall there were fewer than ten who were willing to exert the energy or time to see this project to its final completion, even though others had voted in favor of it.

Several of our members who knew real estate rules furnished leads on available properties and buildings. Finally we were fortunate in finding the present location. The property consisted of an old building with parcels of land on each side that could be used for parking. We initiated an offer to the owners and eventually we purchased it.

With the help of Roy Meadows and Grady Powers (now deceased), the first members who volunteered to help with the construction of the building, we met regularly at the site to haul debris away because the property needed clearing before any building could be accomplished. Overgrown with tall grass and weeds, it had been used for many years as a collection place for trash, including junk automobiles and pieces of many items.

Also on this land was a smaller old building constructed of tin and rotting timbers. There were many pieces of debris surrounding this building making the area look like a dump.

We went over the property carefully in preparation for the building project. We had visions of using the old cinder block building and making repairs to that but there were some obvious faults we would have to work around.

We believed that the tile on the old building floor could be chipped away and replaced with new tile, provided the concrete under the tile was solid. Then we discovered the cinder blocks crumbling and the roof falling into the lower part of the building. The building had been left unattended for many years and the weather had taken its toll on the walls and roof. Therefore we began tearing out the non-usable items and transporting them to the dump.

We decided to become our own contractor and obtain prices from subcontractors. This method worked very successfully although it required someone from the chapter and the building committee to be present until the job was completed.

Eventually other members joined us and remained with the job to the end including M.E. Cozzens, Richard Scherberger and Jackson Goodfellow (now deceased) who furnished machinery for much of the excavation and roof installation for which we were grateful. Several other members appeared on the job site a number of times, even if for only a few minutes.

Finally after eight months of hard labor including dealing with contractors, workmen and other persons, we completed the building. During the entire construction period the support of our members was fantastic, as they took the time to give their input, offer constructive criticism and interview many company employees to get at the bottom of any dispute.

Without the income from the thrift store we could not have constructed our headquarters building. Still, it is not the most elaborately-built structure. Income was limited when we began because the thrift stores were not selling many items. But over the years we have added to it so it now serves our purposes quite well.

We have allowed other veterans' organizations to hold meetings in our building, including a chapter of Vietnam veterans who have met there rent-free for many years. We also allowed the Hampton Roads veterans organization that sponsored the Memorial Day and Veterans Day parades to meet free of charge at our headquarters and our members participated in these parades each year. We alternated the parades between Norfolk and Virginia Beach on a yearly basis until Norfolk required us to pay a fifty-dollar fee for a permit to hold a parade and to confine it to certain streets. This became a burden and we ultimately discontinued the parade in Norfolk.

Finally, an End to Pain and Suffering

In 1960 following the refusal of the VA doctors to treat me for my low-back problems, an orthopedic surgeon in Norfolk examined me. He diagnosed a misalignment of my hips and prescribed a corset brace and a built-up shoe for my left foot, stating that the condition could only have been caused under rare circumstances, such as in wartime.

The VA doctors refused to dispense pills for my pain stating that it would go away eventually without medical treatment. Then when I submitted the paperwork from the orthopedic surgeon including his recommendations for treatment, the VA informed me in no uncertain terms that it would not authorize this expense because I was not qualified to receive the treatment.

I bore the cost to alter my left shoe until about 1984, while the VA doctors refused to assist me. Finally in near disgust, I visited the orthopedic clinic at the Veterans Administration Medical Center (VAMC) in Richmond in an attempt to get relief.

There after I related my history and described my pain, a physician from the Medical College of Virginia who was assisting at the clinic diagnosed my condition as specifically service-connected. He also agreed with my local physician that I required a corset-type back brace and a knee brace to ensure that I would walk relatively upright. This was about eighteen years after I was discharged from the military.

Following the Richmond visit, the Hampton VA provided me with built-up shoes but they were not the correct width. "One size fits all" was the policy and I was informed to use them or buy my own. The built-up shoes were required to keep my hips aligned and support my posture according to orthopedic surgeons.

I have lost time and funds and have gained nothing in my dealings with the VAMC in Hampton. The personnel there procrastinates in every way possible in dealing with disabled veterans who are suffering pain. However I continue to fight for what is rightfully mine, even if it is slow in coming. Hopefully this will come before I die.

In the summer of 1994, I kept an appointment at the Hampton VAMC regarding my lower back pain. This time a physician took an interest in my condition. He made a through examination of my back, which was hurting as usual, as it had been since 1945. He processed the paperwork for an MRI that had to be completed at the Richmond VAMC because Hampton did not have that machine.

In my opinion, this is unfortunate. Most qualified doctors depend upon this procedure. VA literature encourages veterans to visit the VA for medical care, knowing full well that Hampton lacks the necessary equipment for physicians to make the correct diagnoses.

In writing a prescription for the MRI, the VA physician also requested that a neurosurgeon read the results to confirm his diagnosis of a misaligned vertebra he had noticed from a CT Scan. He told me he needed a specialist to verify his diagnosis.

There was a delay of almost two months after the appointment was made because so many patients require the MRI procedure. Then after an examination and review of the MRI film, the neurosurgeon informed me that a piece of bone pressing against my nerves was causing me to have the severe pain.

He believed that a hard blow on my back caused the bone to press unduly against my spine. To prevent further damage, he wanted to admit me that same day for an operation on my back. But when I requested a second opinion, he agreed.

I returned to the doctor at the Hampton VAMC to discuss the operation. He suggested that I consider the travel time to and from Richmond as part of my final decision because of the pain following the operation.

Over a period of weeks I asked questions regarding back surgery of two or three other physicians, fully aware that the VA, despite its claims of assisting disabled veterans, would not pay for the operation in another medical facility, even if the disability to be corrected is service-connected.

Finally I selected Dr. Peter M. Klara who, after reviewing the MRI, agreed with the conclusion that my pain was the result of a severe blow to my back, causing the bone to grow toward the spinal cord. Using diagrams and medical books, he explained what I should expect from the operation if I chose to become his patient. He said he would chip away bone from my vertebra to relieve the pressure on the nerve, which in turn would relieve most of my pain. Finally, he would insert screws in my L-4 vertebra for a more rigid fusion.

In September 1995, Doctor Klara performed the operation at Leigh Memorial Hospital in Norfolk. That operation took away almost all of the original pain I had been suffering for the past fifty years. However now I cannot bend sideways or backward possibly because Dr. Klara placed metal and screws in my vertebra to support my weight and allow the joint to fuse together. I cannot lift many objects, nor can I become gainfully employed in many jobs, even if I wanted to work. But most of the pain is gone.

Some of the VA medical personnel were not happy with me for seeking outside medical care. But I decided that I would be unable to ride from the VAMC in Richmond to Norfolk - a distance of one hundred miles – within three or four days following the operation if it had been performed there. As it was, I suffered excruciating pain following the operation when I was transported in an automobile for only ten minutes from the hospital to my home.

If I had to ride for an hour and a half from Richmond, I would have been devastated to say the least. I still cannot understand why the veteran and especially the disabled veteran must undergo this type of agony when the VA has a hospital in Hampton and only needs to staff it with specialists to afford the proper medical care.

The VA's original purpose was to assist veterans, especially disabled veterans, in obtaining medical care and compensation. Maybe I continue to be a dreamer when it comes to government agencies helping those who have placed their lives on the line in time of war and are in need of proper care.

In 1998 four years after Dr. Klara performed my back operation, I was directed to a new doctor at the VA. He declared that I did not need the built-up shoe because the operation had corrected my condition. He did not examine me but made this diagnosis by looking at my back from across the room.

He and the other doctors present directed me to a shoe warehouse, saying this would be the best place for me to replace my shoes. I spent over three hundred dollars on new shoes, believing the doctor was correct. Now I refuse to talk to him.

For about two months, I had no additional pain in my back but by July 1998, I was again having pain in my lower back so excruciating that I could not walk, sit or sleep. All I could do was suffer.

Finally in desperation, I made an appointment with the new orthopedic surgeon at the VA in Hampton who was there on a part-time basis for two days each week. Following a CT scan of the L5 vertebra, he advised me that I had a herniated disc and he secured an appointment for me with a neurosurgeon at the Richmond VAMC advising him that another operation had to be considered to relieve my pain and correct my condition. At the same time he made arrangements for me to receive steroid shots to ease the pain.

Two months later and still in pain, I was examined in Richmond by a doctor who had no nametag, did not introduce himself to me and for reasons unknown to me, appeared anxious to depart the examining room. After reviewing the CT scan, he denied seeing anything wrong with my back.

Stating he wanted to check with his colleague to be sure both observed the film the same way, he left the room. When he returned, he said he believed the screws and the plates in my back were causing my problem and needed to be removed. I asked him if there were any discs that had bulged out or were herniated. He said he saw nothing wrong with the other vertebrae in my back. After he made this statement, I requested a second opinion and asked to be excused from his care.

The day after this examination I visited Doctor Klara in Norfolk taking the CT scan film with me. He agreed with the original diagnosis and pointed out the problem to me. In the August 1998 operation, he had inserted Ray's Cages between my L-5 vertebrae. He advised me never to have the screws removed from my back unless it could not be avoided.

He explored the possibility of me seeking treatment at a pain clinic in Portsmouth and made appointments for me to have the nerve ends in my lower back near the L-5 vertebrae deadened to reduce the pain. This clinic has reduced the pain in my lower back and made it possible for me to become mobile enough to make life livable.

Doctor Klara also made a written request, which I delivered to the VA, for me to undergo warm or hot bath treatments for my comfort but this never came about. Additionally, he stated that I should consider a morphine pump to relieve the pain in my back. As of this writing, I have not had this procedure done because I am concerned that the morphine pump may erupt following any type of accident.

In 1999 I sought and obtained another appointment with the senior physician at the Hampton VAMC who took measurements of my legs, including the height of my hips. Then he said that I required the built-up shoes that had been taken from me. He completed a written order to the orthotic section to have the shoes I needed made for me, along with other medical equipment to reduce the pain I was suffering.

I told him that I considered it foolhardy, confusing and capriciously self-serving of the other physician to deny me built-up shoes at that first examination. Any physician, regardless of his specialty, should make his decision on treatment for the veteran only after thorough examinations.

This is not done by VA doctors as a general rule because there are no specific guidelines except to get the patient in and out of the office as soon as possible. It is the numbers game. The physician gains because he has seen more than his share of patients that day but in the end the patient loses because he is given pills to mask his difficulty.

My contact with the VAMC at Hampton has been with the supervisor, who has been very careful in treating me after I informed him of the conditions I suffered previously.

Although I have made some scurrilous remarks regarding VA physicians and the medical care they offer, this does not excuse Congress, which has not done a laudable job funding the necessary medical treatment for disabled veterans. In fact, Congress permits the bureaucrats within Veterans Affairs to get a larger share of the funds without ensuring that these funds are spent on the proper care of veterans such as hiring enough physician specialists to carry out the responsibilities the VA promises to fulfill.

The VA policy should be to treat the patient as a dependent infant, in a manner of speaking, whose needs must be cared for until it is determined that his malady is either cured or is not service-connected. Instead, at no time have disabled veterans received the medical care, education, on-the-job training or other benefits due them without harsh delays and at times, threats by the hospital staff.

Additionally for the past few years, Congress has reduced the funds to care for disabled veterans and in a way ignored them at the expense of those who are not disabled. Then Congress questions the resentment disabled veterans feel.

As a small example, during the 1950s, my compensation was reduced from the great amount of 30% down to 10% because, according to the legislators who inserted their own pork into every bill they submitted, there were not sufficient funds to pay the federal government's bills.

If the truth were known, my rating should have been at least 70% before the reduction. I based this percentage on my disabilities and especially on the much higher ratings of military personnel today. Some of them were involved in civilian automobile accidents that caused broken bones and other injuries, which I regret; but under the present-day laws made by Congress, these veterans are entitled to more funds than I receive from service-connected injuries.

The VA physicians and adjudication boards decide these cases. These agencies are applying pressure upon disabled veterans to forget their pains, ignoring these wounded veterans without consideration of their conditions. Unfortunately, there are not sufficient numbers of disabled veterans complaining to Congress about our inadequate medical care.

The following information is intended to further explain the medical situation at the Hampton VAMC. However, it must be interpreted in a way to help other disabled veterans receive proper medical care. I will not name the persons I describe in these incidents, nor do I wish to cause hurt feelings to those who are trying to do their jobs properly.

A number of years ago, I became friends with an elderly man – a watchmaker living near my home. He visited the VFW Post across the street from his house. Over a period of about two years, I would take him food and go to the grocery store for him because his age prevented him from driving himself around town. He'd been married but I never learned what happened to his wife.

My friend began to build a new house for himself on his property. Upon completion of the new house, he resolved not to move in for another month, electing to remain in the old house, which was about to fall down. One day the real estate agent, who'd gone by to see him, called me to inform me that the old house had burned.

I discovered that my friend had been taken to a local hospital with life-threatening injuries. I took the responsibility of calling the VA to inform them that he was eligible to be transferred the VA in Hampton because of his disability. Accordingly, he was transferred there for additional treatment.

One day I decided to visit him to determine if he was in need. As I was walking toward his room, I heard loud cursing which suddenly stopped when I entered the room.

I learned a little later it was an unidentified staff person using the foul language toward my friend who was helpless, not really knowledgeable of his condition or where he was at that time and unable to hear properly, which was part of his disability. I reported the incident and talked to the director of the hospital about it as well but to my knowledge nothing was ever done to discipline this staff member or to correct the situation.

Following my friend's death, I again went to the director to get an explanation and learn the identity of the culprit but I was dismissed with a scowl and admonished because I was not a relative.

Later, patients in the spinal cord ward told me how the staff, upon whom they were dependent for all of their movements, had taken advantage of them. They stated that they were taken out of bed around 7 a.m. and not returned until around 8 to 9 p.m. After I spoke with the physician in charge, this mistreatment was corrected and the patients now are back in bed in two to three hours.

Once, when a patient was dropped on the floor, the staff person laughed about it and made no report of the bruises caused to the patient. Another patient informed me that his family mailed cheese to him but since he was not able to cut the cheese, the staff consumed the entire package, leaving him nothing.

Another patient was forced to stay out of bed as punishment because he requested food. One patient informed me that staff members were taking food items from the delivery trucks near the kitchen and placing them in personal automobiles. This was reported but nothing was ever done to stop the thievery, which may still be going on.

Another patient informed me that patients were refused food for periods of time just to punish them for not doing what the staff wanted. During this punishment, staff members, including nurses, would laugh and make fun of the patient who was not able to defend himself or herself.

The foregoing is just a small sample of the trouble at the Hampton VAMC and may very well be the reason disabled veterans do not want to be admitted there. However, most of the physicians are dedicated to trying to help the patients. There are only a few who could care less and are waiting for quitting time and payday or the rotation to end for them. Is this a way to treat disabled veterans there or at any hospital?

My Quest for Liberty and Justice

My intention has been to inform those who have no knowledge of the Great Depression of the 1920s and 30s, the beginning of World War II with Japan and Germany or the hardships endured by those who suffered through those grueling years.

Before the war, most of us had to work or starve and we chose the former, struggling with the help of our families to get by. During the war, the main criterion was to stay alive because dead men cannot fight. However, the pain suffered from actions by the enemy will remain with each of us until we die.

Most of these pains are severe, and in many cases any operation to alleviate them only causes them to be more severe. Medications, which the hospitals and doctors rely on as the principal treatments only mask the pains. Furthermore, most if not all survivors of WW II have aspirations of living forever but sadly we know that will not happen and for a good reason. Ultimately we would like to be respected by our peers.

My experiences emerged from my early years of struggling to survive after an unknown person attempted to destroy us apparently out of jealousy because of my father's employment. Since that horrible night, I have striven to do what I believe to be right – engaging in honest work, defending our country, striving for justice for those who cannot defend themselves and bringing honor to my family and myself. In recounting these experiences, it is my hope that others can learn lessons that will serve them in the future just as the lessons I learned have served me so well.

Share Howard W. Wiseman's adventures with others.

Use this order form or a copy of it to order additional copies of *The Second Wiseman – A Quest for Liberty and Justice*. Groups or institutions wishing to order 10 or more copies qualify for a substantial discount of 60% off the retail price of $18.95, or $7.60 per book.

Please send me _____ copies of The Second Wiseman – A Quest for Liberty and Justice.
Enclosed is a _____check or _____ money order made out to

Wordminder Press for _____.

Number of books	Price	4.5% Tax (Virginia)	Shipping	Total
1-9	$16.95 each		$4.00	
10 or more	$6.78 each		$4.00	

Shipping Address (please print):
Name _____
Address _____

_____

_____
Phone _____
Email _____
(To notify you of shipping date)

Mail order form and payment to:
Wordminder Press
PO Box 10438
Norfolk, VA 23513-0438.